UNDERPINNINGS OF ISLAMIC ECONOMICS BANKING AND FINANCE

DR. MUHAMMAD AWAIS, PHD.
DR. OMAR KHALID BHATTI, PHD.
PROF. DR. IBRAHIM GURAN YUMUSAK, PHD.

AURAQ

Printed in the Islamic Republic of Pakistan.
First Printed: December, 2018
ISBN: 978-969-7868-04-9
Price: Rs 700 PKR, 7$ USD

Islamabad, Pakistan

www.auraqpublications.com | www.kitaabian.com
raabta@auraqpublications.com | +92 300 0571 530
Social Media: @AuraqPublications

FOREWORD

The Author's research on the Islamic Economic, Banking and Finance System is exceptional. They tell an interesting and timely story about the concepts of public finance and wealth within the Islamic culture and today's evolving economy. The book explores the concept of wealth, property and the circulation of money within the Islamic faith and how that process is governed within the faith by the Shariah laws. With the growth of the economy of Pakistan, it helps the reader place that growth in context of the Islamic faith. I truly enjoyed reading the book and know that the readers will find it both informative and interesting.

James Estes, PhD

(MBA, CFP, CLU, ChFC, CPCU)
Professor Emeritus California State University San Bernardino
Department of Finance and Accounting

FOREWORD

Islamic Economics has emerged as a distinct academic discipline during the last quarter of the 20th century. Islamic Economics and Finance is now taught in many universities throughout the OIC member countries as well as in some European universities at the bachelor's, master's and doctorate levels. Despite a number of conferences, seminars, workshops and symposia on Islamic Economics, there is still felt a dire need of research material in a sorted manner for undergraduate students according to their syllabi and courses of studies. The students are often constrained by limited time frame of the semester and therefore have to concentrate only on selected themes.

The need for a standard textbook that should cover the necessary topics in simple, lucid but comprehensive manner has been felt for a long time. The authors have strived to present this book to fulfill this need. The authors have been practically involved in teaching of Islamic Economics and Finance at the university level for quite some time. Their hard work of completing the assigned task with professional rigor is commendable. The authors have followed a comparative approach in the text, explaining the concepts of Islamic Economics and Finance side by side with the conventional economic theory and policy. This approach seems to be appropriate for the primary audience, rather inevitable for a better understanding of Islamic Economics. The readers who are well versed in conventional economics may bypass such details and focus on the Islamic themes without loss of generality. For those who are new to this discipline, this book may prove an excellent source of knowledge in the form of a ready reckoner or a primary desk reference.

Prof. Dr. Ibrahim Sani MERT

Antalya Bilim University, Turkey

PREFACE

The Islamic banking and finance sector has experienced a significant and an extraordinary progression in the last few years. The overall sector has enjoyed a growth rate of 10-15% per year. At present, more than 500 Islamic Banking and Financial Institutions are operating globally, with assets worth more than $1.9 trillion (IFSB, 2016). This massive progress has brought Islamic finance to everyone's attention, prompting the major conventional banks to set up Islamic financial windows in order to cater Muslim customers and also to take an advantage of the growing demand.

With such growing need for Islamic Banking and Finance, it is extremely pivotal to promote a robust and a sound understating about the subject. In fact, the fundamentals of economics, finance, and banking from an Islamic viewpoint must be presented in the simplest manner to improve the overall proficiency and know-how about the subject. Hence, this was the core reason and objective that motivated us to write this book on Islamic economics, banking, and financial system.

This book encompasses the elementary concepts of finance, banking, Islamic economic system, Islamic contract, Profit and loss sharing, Riba, Islamic investment, Asset-backed financing and Islamic modes of financing. As stated earlier, the objective of this book is to present readers with the clearest and easy understanding of the key concepts of Islamic economics, banking and financial system. In addition, this book can be used as a handbook by all of those who are eager to learn the core principle concepts of Islamic Economics, Finance, and Banking.

Finally, we must confess that writing this book is a very difficult task as it took us six years to come with this simple version. We have tried our level best to ensure that there are no errors or mistakes. However, if any inaccuracy detected in the book is purely unintentional and we sincerely seek forgiveness from ALLAH (ﷻ) Who is the most merciful and forgiving.

Dr. Muhammad Awais, PhD.
(Assistant Professor, Foundation University Islamabad-Pakistan)

Dr. Omar Khalid Bhatti, PhD.
(Associate Professor, Istanbul Medipol University- Turkey)

Prof. Dr. Ibrahim Güran YUMUŞAK, PhD.
(Professor, Istanbul Sabahattin Zaim University-Turkey)

TABLE OF CONTENTS

اقرأ

SECTION – 01

ISLAMIC ECONOMIC SYSTEM

This section 'Islamic Economic System' discusses the role of Islam in Public Finance, Concept of Wealth in Islam, Theory of Property in Islam, Factors of Production (FOP's) in Conventional and Islamic System, Characteristics of Wealth Distribution in Islam, and Standard of Wealth Distribution in Islam. This section sheds light on the basics of Sharia laws for the whole economic system.

Role of Islamic Economic System (IES)

Islamic Economic System has the potential to play a vital role in all sectors of the economy both at national and international levels. Some Scholars try to define this system in a different manner without much insight of Islamic Economic System. No doubt Islam is a complete code of life that encompasses all spheres of life of an individual and the society including social interaction of individuals and groups, moral values, economic relations, matrimonial and political affairs etc. In Islam, interest (Riba) is considered abominable and detested because it circulates the money in an erratic manner in the hands of few influential individuals or groups which ultimately leads to monopolies in the economy and selfishness. An interest-based investment, which is prohibited in Islam, is the corner stone of capitalism, in which the investor provides capital to get a fixed amount of profit/ interest on his/ her investment.

Public Finance in Islamic Economic System

Public finance is a significant area of the economic system (Bahl & Linn, 1992). Public finance is a process which deals with the distribution and the provision of financial resources needed for functioning of the government. It is closely linked with the government taxation and its expenditures, in short it deals with the financial aspects of the government.

In Islam, the principles of public finance are derived from the Holy Quran. The practices as well as sayings of Prophet Muhammad (ﷺ) form basic guidelines for the operations of public finance. According to the Islamic system of public finance, the public money must be distributed in an equitable manner (from weaker to stronger) for the purpose of social security and well-being of society.

In early days of Islam, prominent Muslim scholars wrote a number of books on the topic of public finance in the Islamic context. Abu Yusuf, Yahya B. Adam, and Qudamah B. Jafar wrote Kitab al-Kharaj a renowned book on public finance. Furthermore, Abu Ubayd, Humayd Bin Zanjawayah, and Abu Jafar Bin Nasr-al-Dawudi, in their book Kitab al-Amwal, brought forward different theories about public finance. Al-Sultaniyah wrote Kitab al-Ahkam on the same topic.

Public finance is the domain of the state in any economy because financial condition of a single individual is an outcome of the conditions of national economy (as GDP per capita can be used as a proxy for nation's Human Development). Major function of the Islamic economic system is based on arrangements for correct circulation of money.

CHAPTER – 01

THE ISLAMIC ECONOMIC SYSTEM

Islam proclaims that an employee is not only a worker, but also a guardian of all responsibilities and assets placed at his/ her disposal. He/ she would be answerable to ALLAH (ﷻ) for the duties and responsibilities assigned to him/ her.

Economic systems are means by which states allocate funds and manage trade of goods/ services inland and abroad. These are used to regulate the five factors of production which include labor, capital, entrepreneurs, land/ physical resources and information resources. A major function of financial management is circulation of money which ultimately strengthens economic system of a country.

In Islamic Economy, the concept of resources and ownership is different because it is reckoned in Islam that all resources are created and owned by ALLAH (ﷻ) while a person uses/ consumes these resources according to his/ her requirements. Hence, it cannot be declared that available resources are scarce. The problem lies in the fair distribution of resources among the deserving and needy.

There are different types of resources, natural and artificial, our main focus in this chapter is on the

"Distribution of wealth/ resources" which is an important facet of life. Before explaining this point, we shall discuss few major principles which distinguish Islamic and non-Islamic system of economy.

Economic System of Islam

In non-Islamic societies, interest-based investment is the basis of an economy (capitalism) which has become an integral part of the world economy today. In an interest-based investment, normally two parties are involved, one being the "investor" (who provides capital as loan) and the second being the "manager" (who runs the business). An investor's profit is fixed at a pre-determined rate of interest on the investment regardless of the business earning profit or loss. The Holy Prophet (ﷺ) prohibited this kind of interest-based investments and transactions.

To understand interest (Riba) in the language of Quran and Sunnah, following verses of Quran may be taken into consideration:

يَا أَيُّهَا الَّذِينَ آمَنُواْ لاَ تَأْكُلُواْ الرِّبَا أَضْعَافًا مُّضَاعَفَةً ۖ وَاتَّقُواْ اللّهَ لَعَلَّكُمْ تُفْلِحُون

> O ye who believe! Devour not interest involving
> multiple additions, and fear ALLAH (ﷻ) that you
> may prosper. (Chapter 3, Aal-Imran, verse 130)

Islam primarily encourages highest moral values and ethics such as welfare, justice, brotherhood and prosperity for all. Islam discourages the activities by which wealth is accumulated and circulated merely among the rich causing injustice, greed and selfishness, which is why Riba (interest) is strictly prohibited.

Concept of Wealth in Islam

Islam propagates that the sole owner of wealth is ALLAH(ﷻ). He gives right of wealth to a man but the given right is not absolute and boundless. It is arbitrary and regulated by certain restrictions and limitations imposed by ALLAH(ﷻ). One must spend wealth according to the will of the real owner, ALLAH (ﷻ).

ALLAH (ﷻ) says in The Holy Quran:

> "Seek the other world by means of what ALLAH (ﷻ) has bestowed upon you, and don't be negligent about your share in his world. And do good as ALLAH (ﷻ) has done good to you and do not intend to spread disorder on the earth" (28:77).

According to The Holy Quran:

> "All credible forms of possessions are created by ALLAH (ﷻ)".

ALLAH (ﷻ) is the creator, he delegates the right of property/ wealth to people. An individual can only sow a seed but for it to become a tree, is the creation of ALLAH(ﷻ). Once a man asked a question from Hazrat Ali(؆) about the autonomy of man in his life. He replied,

"Stand on one leg" as he did so, Hazrat Ali asked him to take his second leg off the ground, and he could not do so. Hazrat Ali (؆) said, "Man has similar autonomy in his life".

In other words, control and autonomy of man has little role in life, ALLAH (ﷻ) has the power and absolute control of everything in the world. Man has to abide by His laid down principles for the wellbeing of human race.

ALLAH (ﷻ) says in the Holy Quran:

> "Have you considered what you cultivate? Is it you who make it grow, or is it We who make it grow?"

Wealth in any form belongs to ALLAH (ﷻ) who bestows upon man the right to take advantage and use it for the betterment of all creatures on the earth.

Theory of Property in Islam

In a conventional capitalist society, an individual may own a property and utilize it as he likes. Similarly, in a communist society, all types of property belongs to the state and its utilization is also controlled by the government. However, the concept of property in Islam is quite different. Although, Islam gives the right of property to a person, yet, the right is not absolute and unconditional. Granting absolute/ unconditional rights creates inequality in the utilization of resources. To benefit all others, the owner of the property is required to give Zakat every year for the property till he owns it.

Factors of Production (FOP's)

According to capitalism, wealth should only be distributed among those parties who can take part in the process of production. In capitalist economies, land, labor, capital, and entrepreneurship are considered vital factors of production. **"Land"** is a natural resource, which can be used as a means of production. Land is a fixed resource one has to use carefully by creating an amalgamation of its natural and industrial uses. **"Labor"** represents the human capital by which one transforms natural resources and raw materials into finished goods. **"Capital"** represents the monetary resources which are used to purchase other natural resources. **"Entrepreneurship"** is a concept essential for economic resources to be transformed into consumer goods by exploiting various business opportunities through innovative ideas.

Wealth is produced by the management of these four factors in a capitalist system handling each factor distinctively. Interest is given on capital, wages are given to labor, rent is given for land and profit is given to the entrepreneur. In the socialist economy, the issue of interest and rent is automatically solved since capital and land are treated as a national property. An entrepreneur is also an economic resource in the socialist system, so the profit earned by an entrepreneur is not theoretically debatable. Labor alone is considered as a wealth under socialist system and is given wages as compensation for its utilization.

CHAPTER – 02

CHARACTERISTICS OF WEALTH DISTRIBUTION IN ISLAM

There are many characteristics of the distribution of wealth in Islam. Islam has propagated the principle of equality and welfare and suggested a system where wealth is distributed among all tiers of the society. In the absence of Islamic principles, one major problem faced by the world economy is poor wealth distribution. The sole reason for all the disputes/ issues in a society is frustration of the deprived factions who are a prey of poor wealth distribution, adversely affecting the social conditions and materialistic interest of common man.

The Prophet (ﷺ) once said:

"How excellent is having a great wealth in strengthening man's fear of ALLAH (ﷻ)".

The Prophet (ﷺ) also said:

"O Lord! Make bread blessed for us. Do not separate us from it. If it were not for bread we would not have kept up prayers, fast, (and) not have discharged our divine duties."

Standard of Wealth Distribution in Islam

The Islamic concept of economy gives a direction and

guides towards fair distribution of wealth and lays down basic standards of living for every individual in the world. A fair distribution will be helpful to an individual as well as the whole society for solution of common economic issues faced by all members of society.

The Holy Quran, the Sunnah, and Fiqh (Islamic Jurisprudence) clearly indicate the path to fair distribution of wealth. As a baseline, main purpose of fair distribution is to provide the world a natural and predictable economic system which allows each individual freedom to perform and to generate more beneficial outcomes fairly and lawfully. For the fair distribution of wealth in Islam, the steps to be followed include:-

- Prohibition of Interest.
- Avoidance of "Bukhal (not spending money even under compulsion)".
- Avoidance of "Israf (immoderateness)".
- Prohibition of monopoly of private firms.
- Judicious payment of Zakat.

Islamic finance desires a system of equally distributed wealth in the economy for which it is necessary to generate a transparent system of supply and demand along with a powerful relationship between the employee and employer. Islam renounces the system of monopoly in which an individual or a group dominates the whole system.

Islamic Economic System (IES) According to Holy Quran

A comprehensive indication of Islamic Economic System is found in the following verses:-

"We have distributed their livelihood among them in worldly life, and have raised some above others in the matter of social degrees so that some of them may utilize the service of others in their work." (43:32)

The distribution of wealth according to Islam is one of the major factors that plays an important role to grant "right" to an individual. As per teachings of Islam, both type of people, those who are involved as well as those who are not involved in the process of production, are entitled to possess wealth (unlike capitalism and socialism).

The Holy Quran narrates:

"In their wealth, there is a known right for those who ask for it and those who have the need for it." (70:24-25)

The right of the poor has been declared as the right of ALLAH (ﷻ), according to the Holy Quran:

"And pay what is rightfully due to Him on the day of harvesting." (6:142)

Another purpose of the above mentioned teaching is to ensure a proper distribution of wealth between the poor and the rich, in contrast to being controlled by a small group of wealthy individuals and families. Islam discourages an individual or a group to monopolize wealth in the society.

CHAPTER – 03

FACTORS OF PRODUCTION (FOP'S) IN ISLAM

In today's world, people are facing numerous difficulties due to non-implementation of Islamic laws, rules, and regulations. Rich is becoming richer and poor ever poorer indicating failure of capitalism and socialism. The Shariah laws are beneficial for Muslims and non-Muslims all over the world, as Islam is the only religion which strongly advocates systematically helping the unprivileged classes of the society that are in desperate need of monetary help.

Insufficient funds and resources are considered great hindrance in the traditional economies. It is basically implied that the assets are somewhat limited as compared to the liabilities/ wants/ needs which are infinite. But, this principle uses the expression 'wants' in a universal sense which encompasses both the necessities and the luxuries that general public usually wish to have. Money itself has no fundamental worth being not a rentable asset/ tradable product as per the principles of Islam. If the capital/ investment is connected with labor, profit will be generated which is lawful, but if the capital only is used to generate profit, it would be interest which is not halal/ Lawful in Islam.

Factors of Production (FOP's)

FOP's are the inputs used for the purpose of production. There are basically four factors of production (FOP's):

- **Land** is primary asset whose value will not reduce in the near future. Land is a combination of natural resource (water, gas, copper, coal, oil, etc.). It will be provided by the owners to the business for production purposes to which the owners will get rent from the business/ firm. David Ricardo, in "The Principles of Political Economy and Taxation (1821)", stated what came to be known as the classical view: "rent reflects the scarcity of good land".
- **Labor** is mostly the physical as well as mental (technical) efforts of humans to produce finished goods for society in exchange for wage or salary.
- The third resource required is called **capital** which has the ability to be converted into cash/ liquidity. The outcome of the utilization of capital is generation of revenue. The business is bound to pay interest on the total amount of capital. There are many types of capital like fixed, working, financial, etc.
- **Entrepreneur** is an individual who runs a business for the purpose of generating revenue. Entrepreneurs use other FOP's (Land, Labor and Capital) for the production process in order to make a profit. For entrepreneurial venture, time and situation is very important. The efficient entrepreneur has the ability to exploit the time and market in favor of his business venture by innovations.

The FOP's can also be classified into four Ms:

- Money
- Management
- Machines
- Materials

The level of output is generally based on the level of input and the relationship between these inputs and outputs is called the production function. The inputs are starting points and outputs are ending points of the production process. Factors of Production are primary inputs used for production process while raw materials and energy are secondary factors for production. These Factors of Production are considered as building blocks for an economy.

> According to **Prof. Benham**, "Anything that contributes towards output is a factor of production."

It would be impossible to produce any good/ product without any of the four FOPs.

Factors of Production (FOP's) in Islam

In Islam, there are three Factors of Production instead of four, which are:-

- **Land** is a property, if it is owned by an individual, then any natural resources which are discovered from it are shared between the owner and the state by a ratio of 80:20, as according to the Islamic law, $1/5^{th}$ of the natural resources discovered are paid to the state in the form of tax of these resources. The Holy Quran explains:-

  "Know that whatever of a thing you acquire, a fifth of it is for ALLAH (ﷻ), for the Messenger, for the near relative, and the orphans, the needy, and the wayfarer... "(8:41)

- **Labor** is the human force which performs all physical and mental tasks in order to generate revenue and get wages for their services.
- The Islamic perspective of **capital** is different. As per Islam, **capital** is used in production process of business and it cannot be further leased. In simple words, capital as per Islam, is only in the form of cash.

Responsibility of Employer

- **Prophet** (ﷺ) said: "Give the laborer his wages before his sweat dries." [Ibn-e-Majah]
- **Prophet** (ﷺ) said: "Those are your brothers [workers under you] who are around you; ALLAH(ﷻ) has placed them under you. So, if anyone of you has someone under him, he should feed him out of what he himself eats, give him clothes like what he himself puts on, and do not put so much burden on him that he is not able to bear, [and if that be the case], then lend your help to him." [Bukhari]
- **Prophet** (ﷺ) said: "I will be foe to three persons on the Last Day: one of them being the one who does not give dues to the servant he employs even after he has fulfilled his duty." [Bukhari]

So, not only the efficient use of Factors of Production is mandatory, it is also obligatory to give the rights of labor to them in an efficient way.

SECTION - 02

ISLAMIC FINANCING AND BANKING

In this section the topics of Sharia compliant financing, Sharia based financing, project financing, history of conventional banking and its role and responsibilities, features of banking, loan granted by commercial banks, history and aim of Islamic banking and features of Islamic banking have been discussed. This section sheds light on the roles and responsibilities of banking system along with a differentiation of operations of Islamic and conventional banking systems.

Finance

An important aspect of economic and business activities in the world is "finance". Finance can be described as the process of investing, funding, purchasing, and providing sufficient amount of capital for a business activity. It is also the process of enabling the desired flow of money which is beneficial to the whole system.

How is Finance Important in Life?

Finance assists individuals, organizations and businesses in allocation of monetary resources over a certain period of time. Without finance, any trade, industry or commerce cannot run successfully because it is the life line for all of them. In finance, the investor invests capital by taking risk in all circumstances which may be certain or uncertain. The "time value of money" is the decisive factor in profitability of a business and for taking all capital financial decisions. The money (cash) is a depreciable asset because the value of money is more today than that of tomorrow.

Finance is the art of passing currency from hand to hand until it finally disappears. (**Robert W. Sarnoff**) The importance of finance in modern society is similar to importance of oxygen for humans. Despite oxygen being polluted, it is still necessary for human life. In the same way, whether the financial services are interest-free or polluted by interest, they are mandatory for all businesses.

> From Hazrat Abu Hurairah (؏): The Prophet Muhammad (ﷺ) said: "There will certainly come a time for mankind when everyone will take Riba and if he does not do so, its dust will reach him." (Abu Dawud, Kitab al Buyu, Bab fi ijtinabi al shubuhat, & Ibn Majah).

Financial institutions play a significant role in everyday life, especially in business operations. Study of finance enables people to make good investment, financial and operating decisions with the help of financial techniques like capital budgeting etc.

Importance of Finance in Business

Finance is the basic ingredient and driving force of businesses and is pivotal in three major facets of business activities/ practices. Firstly, financial practices ensure circulation of capital through financing of business assets generating revenues for the business. Secondly, they also ensure timely increase in capital by enabling good financial decisions for business expansion and growth. Lastly, financial practices help in gaining maximum amount of profits from businesses. Finance is also helpful in establishing and promoting/ expanding a new business, starting a brand and ultimately satisfying customer needs. Conversely, poor financial management can be a cause of downfall of companies which ultimately results in recession in the economy. Furthermore, the global economy is based on financial processes.

Types of Finance

There are three major types of finance: public, corporate and personal. Each type is briefly explained as follows:-

- **Public finance** consists of roles and functions of government in the economy, such as the role of government in resources allocation, income distribution, and formulation of macroeconomic policies.
- **Corporate finance** deals with the financial decisions within an organization, such as monetary decisions and the tools/ techniques used for implementation of these decisions.
- **Personal finance** is used by an individual/ family in order to make their routine saving and spending choices.

Business and Debt Financing

In the course of any business, good management decisions and purposely formulated business strategies can reduce business risks. Most of the businesses follow predictable seasonal patterns which can be forecasted and risk can be determined and managed through appropriate financial decisions. 'Venture Capital Finance' aids in finding best source of funding for startup businesses. After meeting initial startup funding requirements, financial management is necessary, keeping in view the future financial needs of the business, to reduce costs and risks. In the modern era of business, debt financing also plays a critical role and has a strong relationship with international business activities of multinational corporations. The whole cycle of business in the world is based on the "debt financing" at almost all levels.

Debt has become a whole, a part of which we are.
(**Dave Ramsey**)

Banking

History of Banking

The word "Bank" is of European origin and is derived from the Italian word "banco", which means a table or a counter. Banking started in 2000 BC from Assyria and Babylonia. Banking spread from Italy to Europe and then to the entire world. A number of important innovations took place in Amsterdam (Dutch Republic) during the 16th century and in London in the 17th century which played an important role in modernization of banking systems and processes. During the 20th century, developments in telecommunications and computers brought major changes to banking operations that led to a dramatic increase in size and influence of modern banks.

Technology and Banking

For decades, there was only one type of banking but the introduction of ATM could be regarded as a watermark because it heralded a new era of banking system/services as it provided 24-hour services. Now a days, although banks perform their services through an online system which is flexible, time-saving and efficient yet a walk-in banking system is still the most popular type of banking. The Federal Deposit Insurance Corporation (FDIC) was established under the Banking Act of 1933 in the United States and reforms were introduced which were designed to control speculation.

The adoption of technology has led to the following benefits: greater productivity, profitability and efficiency, faster service and customer satisfaction, convenience and flexibility, 24x7 operations and space and cost savings. (Sivakumaran, 2005).

Customers, Investments and Crisis

In the entire spectrum of financial institutions, investment companies, insurance companies and finance companies that generate profit through the flow of money, banks are just one part. Banks cannot make their operations efficient without market segmentation because if banks do not work according to the location/ type of customers they cannot perform efficiently. Crisis in banks mostly occur because of macroeconomic variables and institutional revolutions. Banks play a significant role in global financial competition which causes gradual changes to macroeconomic variables and at times may suffer a drastic sudden change (revolution).

CHAPTER – 04

APPLICATIONS OF ISLAMIC FINANCING

A unique aspect of Islam is that it provides wholesome guidance for every aspects of human life including economic and financial matters. In the same vein, few aspects of Islamic financing are discussed below.

Shariah Compliant Financing

Shariah compliant financing includes all modes of financing that aids a financier to get fixed or variable predetermined return on his/ her investment according to Islamic principles. The modes/ tools of financial operations of Islamic financial system which have replaced conventional modes/ tools are:-

- **Bai Salam** has replaced the concept of agricultural financing.
- **Bai Muajjal** has replaced the concept of the credit sale.
- **Istisna'a** has replaced the concept of the contract of exchange.
- **Ijara** has replaced the facility of leasing under conventional banking.
- **Murabaha** has replaced short-term loans as well as overdraft facility under conventional banking.
- **Diminishing Musharaka** has replaced conventional mortgage.

Shariah Based Financing

In contrast to Shariah Compliant Financing, Shariah Based Financing consists of the transactions according to the rules of Islam. It means the adaptation of Islamic modes of financing on the basis of profit and loss sharing, such as Musharaka and Modaraba.

Musharaka financing in its literal meaning is "sharing" and it is derived from the Arabic word "Shirka", which means a partner. According to the rules of Islamic finance, it is a type of a partnership based on profit/ loss sharing. All parties involved in such transactions are allowed to invest a specific amount of capital and then earn profit or bear loss on the basis of their share. In "Musharaka" the partners are allowed to share not only cash but also in all other forms of assets. The investors will bear the loss according to the ratios of their investment but get profits on the basis of pre-agreed ratio which may be due to retention of some profit for growth/ expansion of the business. In this contract, all investors must participate in operations of the business but equal amount of work is not the condition to be met. Additionally, investors are allowed to hire employees in order to perform their tasks.

Modaraba financing is a type of partnership where one party (Rabb-ul-mal) will provide the capital in the form of cash or any other form of assets and the second partner (Mudarib) will provide services for the management of business on the basis of expertise. In such type of contract, both parties will receive profits in a specified ratio but the loss will only be borne by the investor and the Mudarib will not be responsible for any loss. It is a trust-based contract and the Mudarib will be liable for loss only in case of misconduct, negligence or breach of contract.

Project Financing

This type of financing is vital part of business and involves strategic planning, risk management, analysis of financing mix and finally raising the desired amount of capital/ funds. In short, project financing is a company's long-term planning on the basis of expected cash-flows of its current and future projects. The principles of Musharaka and Modaraba fully comply with project financing. For project financing, either the amount of investment is pooled by the company itself or expertise of any third party is utilized. In this type of financing, the investor will share the loss incurred in the business corresponding to his/ her investment and the partner who separates him/herself from business operations and limits his/ her responsibility of work in the business cannot claim more share of his/ her profit than his/her investment.

The Modaraba agreement is made when the financier (investor) wants to invest in the project without any concern for other investors whereas the Musharaka agreement is solemnized when the investment for the project is shared from all participants and action of other investors can seriously affect the investor. In Musharaka, if one partner does not want to continue then he/ she may detach him/ herself from the business by getting his/ her share back.

CHAPTER – 05

CONVENTIONAL BANKING

A bank is a financial intermediary/ institution that accepts the deposits and then uses those deposits in different types of lending activities through capital markets or some other institutions. It receives money from people who want to save it in the form of deposits and lends it to those who need money as a loan. In general, banks provide different financial services, some of which consist of dealing with money, profit and service orientation, giving advances/ loans, acceptance of deposits, payment and withdrawal, providing guarantee and agency services etc. Banks generate revenue by taking interest, transaction fees and giving financial advice and other financial services. The major source of generating revenue, however, is through getting "interest" on different types of lending.

Now a days, critical situations are more frequently created in the economy and financial systems by global and regional events, consequently, banks have to play an important role. Stabilizing role of banks in the economy, a country is like a shock absorber. Banks, with the passage of time, have innovated and improved a large number of services to satisfy diverse needs of customers at all levels from individual customers to corporate firms. Although, in today's modern era things change with a blink of an eye, however, for banks, the nature of customers and their need for capital remains constant. Banks have to make innovations to meet ever increasing customer demands. During the last 15-20 years, many regulatory and technological changes have influenced the banking industry as a whole.

Conventional and Modern Functions of Commercial Banks

Banks perform several functions which mainly include:-

- Transfer of payments through online banking, internet banking and other means.
- Accepting and lending money in the form of deposits and loans.
- Issuance of cheques and drafts.
- Insurance services.
- Safekeeping of documents and other valuables.
- Cash management and treasury.
- Providing letter of credit, bonds, guarantees, and some other products.

Features of Conventional Banking

Banks can be divided into different types according to their involvement in different types of activities and provision of different services for variety of customer demands. These include:-

- **Central/ Federal/ National banks** control the currency and maintain country's financial stability. If this function of banks is not done correctly, country's economy is likely to sink and running of the country will become difficult for the government. Central banks perform some specific functions like issuance of paper currency, supervising and controlling foreign exchange and dealing with foreign remittances. Central banks work under the rules and regulations of the government as well as international laws and exist as a separate entity and control the circulation of money and regulate interest rates.

- **Retail Banks** are the most familiar type banks and provide saving services to customers by accepting deposits of individuals and pay interest on the same. The collected deposits are lent to those who need it in the form of loan for earning interest on it. They also provide other retail financial services, like: deposit of utility bills, issuance of credit cards, currency exchange, mortgage, lease and hire purchase, etc.

- **Commercial Banks** are the banks that provide a large number of financial services, however, their major role is to assist in expansion of businesses and to maintain the cash flows for the businesses by providing a large amounts of cash. They take money from the general public in order to provide short-term loans to businesses. They provide various types of services like bill of exchange, remittance money from one place to another place and dealing with cheques, bank drafts, pay orders and other instruments.

- **Investment Banks** are banks which trade securities in the financial markets and also give advice and consultation to corporations or businesses on major activities of capital markets such as acquisition and merger.

- **Saving Banks** accept deposits from low-income clients.

- **Industrial Banks/ Development Banks** are banks that help the new as well as existing businesses by providing cash for their establishment as well as expansion. They usually provide long-term loans and invest in manufacturing/ industrial activities. For long term loans they generate cash by issuing bonds and securities.
- **Land Mortgage Banks/ Land Development Banks** are agricultural banks that help in land development. These banks provide loans for the purchase of real estate and have special service packages for customers who want to utilize barren pieces of land.
- **Indigenous Banks** are banks that generate money by collection of deposits from the general public and grant such money in the form of loans to needy persons. They are basically money lenders and are mostly popular in villages and small towns. Their main objective is to help the low-income families and individuals.
- **Co-operative Banks** work like commercial banks. They provide loans to small farmers, lower level/ small-scale industries and salaried employees.
- **Exchange Banks** are the banks that deal in the exchange of different currencies. They help in various activities like sales and purchase of "gold" and "silver", remitting money from one country to another country, trade of import and export and discounting of foreign bills.
- **Consumer Banks** are the banks that provide loans to the general public for purchase of domestic equipment, such as television, washing machines, cars, etc. The consumers can pay the loan in easy installments.

- **Online Banks** are the banks that allow individuals to perform their financial transactions e.g. account opening, transfer of accounts, balance inquiries, bill payments, transfer of money between accounts, stop-payment request, get loan and credit card applications at home via the internet.
- **Phone Banks** provide the facility to perform financial transactions such as checking balance, bills payments and transfer of funds through mobile phone.

The efficiency of the banking system is increasing day by day which is evident from the increasing number of deposits and transactions per day. Furthermore, the banking system provides ease of access to the poor by its wide variety services in all major and minor cities and towns. Banking services are not restricted merely to urban settlements, rather they are expanding rapidly in rural areas as well. Competition among banks is becoming fiercer overtime and the role of banks is increasing in the life of a common man.

Loan Granted by Commercial Banks

Commercial banks provide two basic types of loans:-

- Secured loans.
- Unsecured loans.

Secured loans are loans with a collateral. These types of loans are provided under a security and guarantee. In secured loans, the creditor gives guarantee to the borrower that in case of default by the borrower the creditor will take the possession of an asset (collateral) clearly specified in the loan documents. There are four types of secured loans:-

- Mortgage loans
- Non-recourse loans
- Foreclosure loans
- Repossession loans

A **mortgage loan** is used for the purchase of real estate (property), with specified periods of payment and interest rates. The property is confiscated by the bank in case of default by the borrower.

In **non-recourse loans**, no partners or other related persons are bound to bear the risk of loss. Such types of loans do not allow the financial institutions or a bank to access the borrower's other assets in case of default by the borrower.

In **foreclosure loans**, the banks may initiate foreclosure (auction) proceedings when the borrower fails to fulfill the payments/ return of loan.

In **repossession loans**, the creditor will hold all the rights to a property or an asset until the borrower has made the last payment of returning the loan.

Unsecured loans are not under any collateral. In such loans the lender will rely on the promise of the borrower to pay-back the payment of the loan. These are also known as personal/ signature loans. The following are types of unsecured loans:

- Term deposits.
- Credit cards.
- Payday loans.
- Medical bills.

A **term deposit** is a deposit that is held at a financial institution under certain terms and conditions.

These deposits are for any term extending from a month to a couple of years.

A **credit card** is a card issued by a financial institution giving the holder an alternative to getting money more often than not in accordance with the offer of the institution. Master cards charge interest and are fundamentally utilized for transient financing. Interest typically starts one month after use of money.

A **payday loan** is an advance that you get from a business that is not a bank, generally known as an advance deposit. It is known as a payday credit, in light of the fact that you, by and large, obtain simply enough to traverse to your next payday, whereupon the cash is expected. Payday advance organizations work under a wide range of titles, and may take postdated checks as insurance. For the most part, they charge a high rate of interest for the credit, which puts the investment rate incredibly high; rates may be as high as four hundred percent.

Medical bills are the expenses of diagnosis, cure, alleviation, medication, or counteractive action of illness, and the expenses for medicines for treatment of any part of the body. These costs include restorative medical administrations prescribed by doctors, specialists, dental practitioners and other medical experts.

CHAPTER – 06

ISLAMIC BANKING

History of Islamic Banking

The concept of the Islamic banking originated from Egypt in 1963. It was an outcome of the efforts of Ahmad El Najjar, who negated interest and emphasized the principle of profit sharing according to the rules of the Islam and "Shariah". After 13 years of this development, in 1976, there were 9 Islamic banks in Egypt. The operations or activities of these banks were non-interest-based and they were usually involved in the business of trading. After 8 years of the development of Islamic bank, Nazir Commercial Bank became the first commercial bank in Egypt.

At global level, the first Islamic bank known as "Islamic Development Bank (IDB)" was established in 1974 with the efforts of Organization of Islamic Countries (OIC). At the initial stage, IDB was engaged in inter-governmental activities. With the passage of time, the number of Islamic banks began to increase throughout the period of 1970s, which included the first Islamic private commercial bank – the Dubai Islamic Bank, the Faisal Islamic bank of Sudan (1977) and the Bahrain Islamic bank (1979).

Aim of Islamic Banking

The main aim of Islamic Banking is to conduct banking operations in consonance with the Islamic teachings because modern banking system involves receipt and payment of interest which is not well-matched with the teachings of Islam. A lot of Muslim researchers and economists are working to find a solution to this problem. On one hand, the theoretical work is being undertaken and on the other, practical experience is being gained in running the interest-free banks and financial institutions. Islamic teachings provide a better foundation for organizing the work of Islamic banks.

Riba in The Holy Quran

Holy Quran strictly prohibits interest based transactions. Muslim societies could not keep away from interest-based transactions due to wide spread interest based policies and networks of Western nations.

Prohibition of interest is beyond any doubt as The Holy Quran states:

> O ye who believe! Fear ALLAH (ﷻ) and give up what remains of interest if you are true believers. But if you do it not, then beware of war with ALLAH (ﷻ) and His Messenger; and if you repent, then you shall have your principal; thus you shall not wrong nor shall you be wronged. (Chapter 2, Al Baqara, Verses 278-279)

In the early history of Islam, prohibition of interest was strictly observed in Islamic society, but with the passage of time decline in the observance of religion and spread of western influence, interest based financial practices began to take roots in the Islamic society. Islam does supports innovative modern financial practices, if they are useful for the human society provided they do not conflict with the fundamental teachings of the Quran and Sunnah.

The use of interest based mechanisms in the process of financial management is not acceptable from Shariah point of view. The basic difference between Islamic and Conventional banking is in the "use of interest based mechanisms" which is forbidden in Islam, but trade and reasonable profits from commercial activities are permissible. In consonance with teachings of Islam, Muslim scholars have developed an entirely different banking model in which interest is not used, instead the Islamic financial system relies on profit/ loss sharing.

Introduction of Islamic Banking

Islamic banking system is the system which is based on the law of Sharia and practically its applications are based on Islamic economics principles. According to the laws of sharia, fixed and floating interest rates are strictly prohibited in any type of transactions. However, Modaraba and Musharaka are two forms of profit and loss sharing business modes which were used even before the concept of Islamic Banking. The concept of Islamic banking is based on the dogma that all institutions which functioning in Islamic society should follow the principles of Shariah. Hence, the concept of Islamic banking is derived from the teachings of Islam. Islam allows the continuance of the system of profit/ loss sharing but prohibits all dealings based on Interest.

Features of Islamic Banking

The Islamic banking/ finance has several features, which will be discussed in detail in the "section 10" of this book. These features are:-

Musharaka is a term used in Islamic finance, which means a partnership based on sharing of profit and loss. It is free from the interest and all parties involved in this contract will face business risk.

Diminishing Musharaka is the type of partnership in the purchase of any kind of property or any depreciable asset.

Modaraba is a kind of partnership, where one partner (Rabb-ul-Maal) provides capital and the second partner (Mudarib) manages the capital by providing expertise/ services.

Murabaha is a kind of sale in which, the seller declares actual cost of the product and then sells it to the buyer by adding some markup/ profit with the knowledge of buyer.

Ijarah is a contract, in which the owner of the asset leases out his asset and charges a rental fee on the asset for a specific or pre-determined period of a contract.

Ijarah-Wa-Iqtina is a contract just like an ijarah, but in this contract, the client purchases the leased property at the end of the contract.

Salam is a contract in which, the seller (Muslam Ilaih) will take advance money for an asset from a client (Rabb-us-Salam) and will deliver such asset at a future date.

Wakalah is a contract in which, one person will choose another person (Wakeel) in order to perform activities on his behalf during his life under specific terms and conditions.

Takaful is the group insurance model in which, each member of the group will guarantee each other against any loss by contribution of money through a pooling system.

Sukuk is a type of financial certificate like a bond, which is based on the rules of shariah.

Qard-E-Hassana is a pure interest-free loan which is given on a goodwill basis, in which the debtor will pay only the loan amount to the creditor.

Istijrar is an agreement, where the buyer will purchase the product in different quantities at different times according to pre-specified terms and conditions.

Bai Muajjal is a type of sale which is based on payment in installments. It is also known as credit sale.

Musawama is a type of trading in which, the price of the product is negotiable and the buyer and seller can bargain on price of the product.

Three main sources of funds and four principals were used in earlier Islamic models. The three main sources of funds are:-

(1) The investor's/ bank's share of capital.

(2) Modaraba deposits from clients.

(3) Demand deposits.

The four principal uses of these funds as identified are:-

(1) Modaraba Financing.

(2) Musharaka Financing.

(3) Purchases of Investment certificate and ordinary shares issued to the public and private sector on profit/ loss sharing basis.

(4) Qard-e-Hassana.

SECTION – 03

ISLAMIC CONTRACT

The "contract" is an agreement between two or more parties. The "offer (I wrote up an agreement)" and the "acceptance (Have you signed the deal yet?)" by "competent persons" are the two major elements of contract. The practices, interpretations and implementation of the Islamic laws depends extensively on Islamic banks, investment institutions and the other financial institutions. There are three types of Islamic contracts in terms of financial as well as commercial activities, these are:-

- Contract of trade
- Contract of donations
- Contract of joint venture

"Bay" is an Arabic word that means a deal/ sale in which a possession is exchanged among the buyer and the seller. Contract of trade revolves around the concept of "bay". Before going into the details of contract of trade, purpose of a contract in Islam needs some deliberation.

The major purpose of the Islamic contract is to provide benefit not only to a single wealthy individual but to the whole community, especially the needy. For example, Islam introduces the contract of "Salam" for impoverished members of society, mainly farmers, in order to secure their assets and income. Similarly, all contracts inherently carry the major purpose of public welfare in Islam.

CHAPTER – 07

ISLAMIC CONTRACT

The principles of Islamic laws act as yardstick to analyze the nature of contracts made between two or more parties. In all the Islamic contracts, transaction of Riba is strictly prohibited.

ALLAH (ﷻ) says in The Holy Quran:-

"O you who believe! Fear ALLAH (ﷻ) and abandon your remaining usury if you are indeed believers." (2.278)

Basics of Islamic Contract

With regard to Islamic contracts, some important points to be noted are:-

- A thorough explanation of the duties and the obligations of all participants of a contract (e.g. buyer and seller) should be stated clearly in order to reduce the chances of default in the near future.
- Representations related to the warranties should be mentioned in the deal.
- The clauses related to privacy must be stated in order to guarantee that the parties may maintain confidentiality of information related to the agreement.
- All parties are required to perform their duties religiously.

- The events and terms/ conditions which can cause termination of the contract must be specified clearly.
- In all international contracts, the jurisdictions and the laws which govern the contract must also be specified vividly.
- Parties in the contract will not exploit each other using clauses of the contract.
- Hiding/ Withholding key information which is necessary for the business transaction can be a cause of contract invalidity. Parties involved in the contract must share all relevant information/ business knowledge with each other.
- Riba is strictly forbidden at all stages of contract.
- Any action that leads to lack of trust between the parties should not be permissible.

Rules of Agreement/ Contract

There are four rules to judge the soundness of an agreement/ contract:-

- A condition that is not in favor of the contract but is favorable for one of the participants of contract then such condition has no value and should not be included in the contract.
- Any condition which is favorable for both parties is legal and should be included in the contract.
- A condition which is neither good for any of the participants of contract nor for the contract should be included in the contract because it is for all parties/ individuals and does not benefit a single party/ individual.
- Any type of transaction with non-Islamic conditions have no value and should not be included in contract.

CHAPTER – 08

FIVE KHIYARS

The meaning of Khiyar is an option or choice, which is exercised to cancel or fulfill the contract. It is the concord between the buyer and the seller to select a definite option.

Options in Contract of Sale

In a contract of sale, there are five basic types of Khiyar or options:

- **Khiyar-al-Ayb** is an option of defect. In this option, the buyer has the authority to cancel the contract if he/ she finds at the end of the transaction a defect in the commodity/ product. The buyer can also ask the seller to replace that piece of item or reduce the price of the defective piece. The seller is responsible for providing a piece of goods or commodity without defects.
- **Khiyar-al-Ghaban** is an option of related to the price. In this option, the buyer has the power or right to return the product or cancel the contract if the price of a commodity/ item goes very high relative to the market price of that commodity/ product before completion of the transaction.
- **Khiyar-e-Shart** is an optional condition or an option to repeal a deal of sale which is based on some specific condition. In such type of contract, seller and buyer both at the time of contract can put some specific

condition for fulfilment of contract. The specification of a time period or some other condition is necessary in these types of contracts. If the condition is imposed by buyer then it is known as Khiyar-al-Mushtari, and if the condition is imposed by seller then it is known as Khiyar-al-Bai.

- **Khiyar-al-Ruyah** is also known as an option of inspecting goods/ product. In such type of contract, if buyer purchases a commodity/ product without initial inspection and after careful checkup of the good/ item, the buyer has a right to cancel the contract in case a defect is found.

- **Khiyar-al-Wasf** is also known as an option of the quality. In such type of contract, the buyer has a right to abandon the contract if some specific of characteristics are missing in a product that the buyer desires or if the quality of a product is not according to the buyer's demand. The buyer usually uses this option when a product is not available at the time of making a contract for evaluation/ inspection.

Iqala is the cancellation of a contract in which all parties willingly cancel the agreement. After the fulfilment of a contract, neither of the parties has a right to cancel the agreement. If the buyer wants to cancel the contract, then he/ she must get the seller's permission. In such type of contract, the commodity's price will never change at the time its return.

Prophet (ﷺ) said that:

> "Who does the Iqala with a Muslim who is not happy with his transaction; ALLAH (ﷻ) will forgive his sins on the Day of Judgment."

CHAPTER - 09

SALE

According to the Shariah, the "sale" is the exchange of any good/ commodity/ item against the other good/ commodity/ item of the same value. More precisely, it is the sale of anything for a price, equal to its value, in terms of cash or kind.

Validity of Sale in Islam

In Islam, valid sale is known as "Bai Sahih" and a sale would be valid if specific conditions are fulfilled which are, firstly availability/ existence of the item/ commodity/ good to be sold (Mabe'e), secondly the possession (Qabza), thirdly the contract (Aqd), and lastly the price (Thaman). If the sale is not valid then it is known as "Bai Baatil". On the basis of the Islamic laws, a sale would not be valid if some of the specific conditions are not fulfilled which are consensus of the buyer and seller, conditions of the offer and the acceptance and the condition of the sale of good.

Fasid and Makrooh Sale

If the existing contract of sale is not valid because of some defect then it is known as "Bai Fasid". The consensus on price and willingness of sale of good are the fundamental conditions of the contract as per the teachings of Islam.

In Islam, if the sale is through some coercion or abhorred, it is "Bai Makrooh". Ayatullah Sistani, has brought forward various factors that render a deal as Makrooh in his book

Touzi ul Masael. A deal will be rendered "Makrooh" if it is being executed between the Fajr Prayer and sunrise or if a third party intervenes, or if the dealing parties are not of good character or if the deal is executed immediately after Azan of Jumah.

Types of Sale Contract

There are some common types of sale contracts as given below:-

- **Bai-Istisnaa** is basically the contract of manufacturing. In Bai-Istisnaa, the producer manufactures an item according to the requirements or specifications of the consumer/ buyer. In such type of contract, the seller makes the product after receiving order of the buyer and product is not present/ does not exist at the time of contract.

- **Bai-Surf** is basically the sale of silver, gold and exchange of currency.

- **Bai-Musawamah** is a contract of sale in which the actual cost/ price of a commodity/ item is unknown to the customer.

- **Bai-Murabaha** is a contract of sale in which the price of a commodity/ item is known to the customer and the customer is willing to pay the seller a cost plus agreed profit amount.

- **Bai-Salam** is a type of sale contract in which the buyer pays full amount price in advance to seller and the seller promises to deliver that commodity at some specific future date/ after a specific period.

- **Bai-Muqayyada** is a type of sale in which both parties purchase goods from one another by exchanging their goods but not in exchange for the cash, it is also known as barter sale.

- **Bai-Muajjal** is the sale on credit.

CHAPTER – 10

VALID SALE

On the basis of Islamic laws, a sale would be valid if specific conditions of sale are fulfilled; Presence of an Item/ a Commodity/ Good (Mabe'e), The Possession (Qabza) of item, The Contract (Aqd), and The Price (Thaman).

Item/ Commodity/ Goods to be Sold (Mabe'e)

The "Mabe'e" means, a good/ an item/ a commodity to be sold. In order to execute a sale, a good/ an item/ a commodity must exist or be tangible, has some value and be usable or obtainable.

The Possession (Qabza)

It is condition of having, possessing or acquiring something. The physical possession or the qabza must be materialized for a sale to be valid. In Islamic terms, it is called haqiqi qabza which means the seller presents and delivers the product and the buyer gets the ownership of the item.

The Contract (Aqd)

It is a voluntary, purposeful, lawful and necessary concord among two or more competent person/ groups. The willingness of a person is very important, the buyer may present the product by telling attributes of the product. For a contract, there must be a buyer and seller and both must have the ability to understand the deal and analyze the conditions, which means that both of them must be sensible and mature (competent). The essential conditions for the sale transaction to be completed are:-

1) Transaction must be instant.
2) Transaction must be non-conditional.

The Price (Thaman)

It is the amount of money predictable, necessary or known in compensation for some item. From the perspective of applicability, free will and quantification is important.

SECTION – 04

PROFIT AND LOSS SHARING

Introduction of Profit and Loss Sharing

Profit and loss sharing is a technique used in Islamic banking in order to eliminate interest. This technique, in abbreviated form depicted as PLS (Profit and Loss Sharing), entails sharing of risk and returns by two or more parties engaged in a business. In the business of banking, usually three parties/ groups are involved - the users of financial resources, the bank which provides funds to the users and provides financial advice/ facilitation, and the third party/ group is savers/ owners of money.

PLS in Islam

Islamic banking system utilizes a variety of practices and techniques which do not entail taking or giving interest. The Islamic financial system propagates the idea of contribution in a business deal backed by operational assets and using financial resources on a PLS basis. Such interest free participatory forms are known as Musharaka and Modaraba.

CHAPTER – 11

FUNDAMENTALS OF MODARABA

History of Modaraba

It is a very old form of financing used by the Arabs from ancient times long before the advent of Islam. Modaraba suited the Arabs of Mecca according to their culture and traditions. They themselves were traders, transporting goods to the north towards Syria in summer and to the south in Yemen in winters. They purchased products from their homeports for inland transportation to other cities for selling and used the money from sale for purchasing products for taking to their home towns or for re-sale abroad to a different destination.

Introduction of Modaraba

It is a type of partnership, in which one partner known as "Rabb-ul-mal" provides cash and the second partner known as "Mudarib" gives his/ her services. Subsequently, the business profits are shared based on a pre-decided ratio. In ancient times, businessmen who had their own capital, enjoyed the entire profit from their business. But, those who used the capital of investors, had to share the profits with investors according to predefined/ pre-decided ratio of profit sharing. Similarly, the intermediary agents who carried the goods of others had to offer profits to their principals after taking their own share of profit.

This type of business was regulated by local laws and traditions and was known by the name Modaraba.

Modaraba through Investment Only

In this type of contract, the investor usually provides capital and the authority to make all necessary business decisions to the Mudarib who ensures smooth operations of the owner's business. Also, the investor has the right to oversee the actions of the Mudarib and work with him with his permission. In Modaraba, the liquid amount of an asset (cash) is the usual form of capital but other assets such as land and equipment etc. can also be considered as capital if these are assessed in terms of their value.

Types of Investment

In general economic system, there are two types of investments:-

- **Active Investment.** In this type of investment, the entrepreneurs invest their own money and then manage all operations of the business.
- **Passive Investment.** In this type of investment, people invest their money but do not take part in operations of the business and enjoy only a specific percentage of profit. Some examples are, depositing money in the bank in returns for a fixed amount of interest payment, purchasing shares of a company in order to get dividends and buying a company's bond for coupon payments.

Investment in Islam

In the Islamic financial system, actively-managed investment is totally permissible which rewards an individual's struggle and investment. Passive type of investment is also permissible which rewards investment and taking the share of profit by passive investors from net profit which is allowed. However, any type of investment that earns profit by taking interest on loan, is forbidden in Islamic financial system.

There are two types of Modaraba:

- **Al Modaraba Al Muqayyadah.** It is also known as restricted Modaraba. The investor initially specifies a particular type of business and a particular place for the business operations and then invests the money in that business.
- **Al Modaraba Al Mutlaqah.** Known as unrestricted Modaraba in which investor give the capital to the mudarib (asset manager) who has the liberty to invest that capital in a legal business most suitable for the provider of the capital/ investor. However, the mudarib, who has the authority to make operational decisions of the business cannot lend money to any third party without the investor's permission. The mudarib is also not authorized by investors to:-
  1. Invest their money in any other business without consent of the investor.
  2. Keep one or more co-workers/ partners.

Modaraba Expense

In such type of contract, the Mudarib shares the agreed ratio of profit with the investor, but his expenses like transport, wear and tear of equipment, medical expenses and meals are not included in the Modaraba. Nevertheless, if Mudarib is traveling for business, his boarding, lodging and transport etc. will be treated as business expenses. If Mudarib leaves for a voyage which composes Safar-e-Sharai (more than 48 miles) but does not stay overnight, his costs will not be borne by the Modaraba.

Distribution of Profit and Loss

It is essential for the soundness of the Modaraba that both parties agree, right at the start, on a clearly stated ratio of profit. The Shariah has fixed no exact ratio and it has to be mutually decided by free will of both parties. They can divide their share in the same percentages according to the percentage of their capital or time and efforts made by Mudarib. In most of cases both parties share the profit equally computed at 50:50 ratios.

The investor and Mudarib cannot set a fixed amount of profit for each other and cannot fix the amount of income on the basis of capital either. Separately from agreed upon profit sharing ratio, as decided in the above approach, the Mudarib cannot argue any monthly pay or a charge or compensation for the effort done by him.

Roles of the Mudarib

- **Ameen (Trustee):** To take care of the capital maturely except natural calamities/ disasters.
- **Wakeel (Mediator):** To manage the finances offered by the investor.
- **Shareek (Partner):** Division and sharing of profits.
- **Zamin (Answerable):** To be held responsible for all acts on his part.
- **Ajeer (Worker):** When the Modaraba is rendered invalid (fasid) due to any reason, the Mudarib is permitted to only the wage, Ujrat-e-Misl.

Termination of Modaraba

This contract will terminate at the time of its expiry. It can also be terminated when both parties lose trust on each other and are not willing to continue the contract.

CHAPTER – 12

FUNDAMENTALS OF MUSHARAKA

Introduction of Musharaka

It is a type of partnership, where each partner contributes in investment and skills. In the Islamic system of finance, Musharaka or Sharika or Shirkat (Arabic: مشاركةor ركة) means a business association, in which capital is provided by two or more parties for establishment and running a business. Banks can also take part in provision of capital along with support in terms of advice or other financial services. The profits are distributed among the parties on basis of quantum of their investment or at a pre-decided ratio, similarly, loss is also shared accordingly. Musharaka and Modaraba can overlap in certain situations where all the interested parties provide capital to the mudarib and modaraba becomes musharaka, actually all the parties take the benefit of experience of mudarib. The loss in case of modaraba is not the liability of the mudarib whereas in musharaka, mudarib also shares loss with others. Musharaka and modaraba are in fact joint ventures with profit and loss sharing in business as a part of Islamic Financing rather than interest bearing loans which is an essential part of exploitative capitalism.

Significance of Musharaka

Under Islamic laws, musharaka implies a joint venture structured for business by more than two parties in which participants share the profit and loss in an agreed upon ratio which is generally proportional to the quantum of investment by each party. Musharaka is a present-day term that is synonymous with Shirkah. Musharaka is a kind of Shirkat-ul-Amwal which means sharing capital for a business. Musharaka has broad ramifications for Islamic banking and gives an incredible option to the investment-based economy.

The Basic Rules of Musharaka

Since Musharaka is an agreement/ contract, all conditions and principles of an agreement/ contract must be met. Furthermore, there are some essential terms that are particular to Musharaka, explained in the ensuing paragraphs.

Appropriation of Profits

The extent of profit to be distributed among the parties must be decided at the time of agreement/ contract. As per Imam Malik and Imam Shafe'i, it is important that each party's share in the profit is precisely equivalent to the extent of provided capital in the business/ organization.

Appropriation of Losses

All Muslim law specialists unanimously agree that each party's share in the loss must be precisely equivalent to the quantum of provided capital. Anything other than this distribution of profit/ loss will render the agreement invalid.

Administration of Musharaka

As a standard procedure, in musharaka, every party is required to take part in the administration of organization/ business. Each party is equally responsible for operation of the business/ organization and effort of one party should be recognized by others. All parties, with mutual consent can also decide to hire on contract any other individual or party for the administration of business/ organization.

End of Musharaka

It is a consensus by legal scholars that an organization/ business being run through musharaka is dissolved if:-

- o One of the participants decides to dissolve the organization/ business.
- o One of the participants breaches the trust of others.
- o One of the participants becomes mentally impaired.
- o In case, remaining participants want to continue the business under any of the above situations, it is possible with shared understanding. The remaining parties would need to buy the share of the quitting/ exiting partner.

CHAPTER – 13

FUNDAMENTALS OF DIMINISHING MUSHARAKA

According to this form of business, an owner and his tenant/ manager take part either in the joint responsibility for a property or in a joint business. The share of the tenant/ manager is divided into installments who with the passage of time gradually acquires the business by purchasing it from the owner in full.

As a participatory mode with profit and loss sharing, Musharaka is considered to be the most coveted mode of Islamic financing. Diminishing Musharaka is presently being utilized broadly within numerous areas of financing depreciable assets, for example, mortgage and auto loans.

Home Financing Transactions under Diminishing Musharaka

The transactions usually include making a joint proprietorship in the purchase of property, whereas loan from the Islamic bank is offered to a customer for this purpose for a specific time. For instance, a bank may finance 90% of the total price, whereas the Buyer invests 10% of the total cost. The customer provides guarantee to the bank and periodically pays back the remaining installments over a specific period of time so that the said property may be purchased. The borrower will pay the monthly installments for maximum of 20 years to become the sole owner of the said property. The customer buys a pre-agreed portion of the bank's share in the property, thus expanding customer's possession in the property and lessening bank's share by a comparative sum. The rental paid on the bank's share is balanced as per the bank's decreasing share and the transaction closes with the exchange of ownership for the whole property to the customer at the end of lease term.

SECTION - 05

RIBA

Riba could be roughly deciphered as "Usury". Riba is illegal in Islamic Financial Laws (Fiqh) and is considered as a sin. Essentially, it is undesirable for material gains in a business.

While the expression "Riba" is regularly equated with "Enthusiasm" by a lot of people, the Qur'an really depicted "Riba" as a general term that is not just restricted as a monetary term.

There are two sorts of Riba explained by legal Islamic scholars, a built in profit from a loan without any administration or effort (Maisir) which is denied by the Qur'an and the second type is product trades in unequal amounts, which is also precluded in the Qur'an. In the Islamic concept, interest means such benefit that is obtained without putting any effort in a transaction. Hazrat Shah Waliullah Dehlvi (رحمةالله), an extraordinary researcher and pioneer, has given an exceptionally compact and exact meaning of investment with Riba. He says,

> "Riba` is a loan/ an advance with the condition that the borrower will come back to the loan provider more than and superior to the amount lent."

CHAPTER – 14

RIBA ACCORDING TO QURAN

Riba is essentially a monetary issue in perspective that all religions and mythologies have precluded, limited, discouraged, disdained, or debased Riba. Each one of the three significant divine (Ilhami) religions i.e., Islam, Christianity and Judaism have firmly censured and denied Riba in its unique forms. Later, the pastors of Jews and Christian Church surrendered the restriction of Riba (interest, usury) that lead humanity into financial and political crises of present era.

The following verse of The Holy Qur'an clarifies this perspective:-

> O believers! Do not devour interest, doubling and redoubling. [3:130]

If we explore Qur'an we come across at least four places where ALLAH (ﷻ) has mentioned interest and instructed not to indulge in it . The first one is in Surah Al-Baqarah verse no.275

> "Those who devour usury will not stand except as stands one whom the Satan by his touch has driven to madness. That is because they say, "trade is like usury", but ALLAH (ﷻ) has permitted trade and has forbidden usury",

In the next verse 276 in the same place, The Holy Qur'an says,

> "ALLAH (ﷻ) will deprive usury of all blessing, and will give increase for deeds of charity, for he does not love any ungrateful sinner."

Two verses later in verse 278 HE (ﷻ) says,

> "Oh you who believe! Fear ALLAH (ﷻ) and give up what remains of your demand for usury if you are indeed believers."

In verse 279 HE (ﷻ) says,

> "If you do not, take notice of war with ALLAH (ﷻ) and his Messenger (ﷺ) but if you repent you shall have your capital sum. Deal not unjustly and you shall not be dealt with unjustly."

In the second place in Surah Aal-Imran, verse no.130 ALLAH (ﷻ) says:

> "Oh you who believe! Devour not usury doubled and multiplied; but fear ALLAH (ﷻ) that you may prosper."

In the third place in Surah Al-Nisaa' ALLAH (ﷻ) states in verse 161,

> "That they took usury though they were forbidden and they devoured people's wealth wrongfully; we have prepared for those amongst them who reject faith a grievous chastisement."

In the fourth place, Surah Al-Room, verse no.39 ALLAH (ﷻ) mentions:-

"That which you give in usury for increase through the property of people will have no increase with ALLAH (ﷻ): but that, which you give to charity seeking the countenance of ALLAH (ﷻ), it is these who will get a recompense multiplied."

CHAPTER – 15

RIBA ACCORDING TO HADITH

Following Ahadith on Riba are significant to understand the whole concept:-

Hazrat Jabir (ﷺ) reported that the Messenger of ALLAH (ﷺ) cursed the devourer of usury, its payer, its scribe and its two witnesses. He also said that they were equal (in sin). (Muslim)

Hazrat Abu Hurairah (ﷺ) reported that the Holy Prophet (ﷺ) said: A time will certainly come for the people when none will remain who will not devour usury. If he does not devour it, its vapor will overtake him. (Ahmed, Abu Dawood, Nisai & Ibn Majah.)

Hazrat Abu Hurairah (ﷺ) reported that the Messenger of ALLAH (ﷺ) said: Usury has got seventy segments. The easiest segment of them is a man marrying his mother. (Ibn Majah)

Hazrat Abu Hurairah (ﷺ) reported that the Messenger of ALLAH (ﷺ) said: I came across some people in the night in which I was taken to the heavens. Their stomachs were like houses wherein there were serpents, which could be seen from the front of their stomachs. I asked: O Gabriel! Who are these people? He replied these are those who devoured usury. (Ahmed, Ibn Majah)

Hazrat Abdullah bin Hanzalah (رضي الله عنه) (who was washed by the angels) reported that the Messenger of ALLAH (ﷺ) said: A dirham of usury that a man devours and he knows is greater than 36 fornications. (Ahmed & Darqutni)

Riba in Hadith

General

From Jabir (رضي الله عنه): The Prophet (ﷺ), may curse the receiver and the payer of interest, the one who records it, the two witnesses to the transaction and said: "They are all alike [in guilt]." (Muslim, Kitab al-Musaqat, Bab la'ni akili al-riba wa mu'kilihi; also in Tirmidhi and Musnad Ahmad)

From Abu Hurayrah (رضي الله عنه): The Prophet (ﷺ), said: "Riba has seventy segments, the least serious being equivalent to a man committing adultery with his own mother." (Ibn Majah)

From Abu Hurayrah (رضي الله عنه): The Prophet (ﷺ), said: "ALLAH (ﷻ) would be justified in not allowing four persons to enter paradise or to taste its blessings: he who drinks habitually, he who takes Riba, he who usurps an orphan's property without right, and he who is undutiful to his parents." (Mustadrak al-Hakim & Kitab al-Buyu')

Riba an Nasiyah

It is defined as excess, which results from predetermined interest (sood) which a lender receives in excess of the principal (Ras ul Maal).

From Usamah ibn Zayd (رضي الله عنه): The Prophet (ﷺ), said: "There is no riba except in Nasiyah [waiting]." (Bukhari, Kitab al-Buyu', Bab Bay' al-dinari bi al-dinar nasa'an, also Muslim & Musnad Ahmad) "There is no riba in hand-to-hand [spot] transactions." (Muslim, Kitab al-Musaqat, Bah bay'i al-ta'ami mithlan bi mithlin & in Nasa'i)

From Anas ibn Malik (رضي الله عنه): The Prophet (صلى الله عليه وسلم), said: "When one of you grants a loan and the borrower offers him a dish, he should not accept it; and if the borrower offers a ride on an animal, he should not ride, unless the two of them have been previously accustomed to exchanging such favors mutually." (Sunan al-Bayhaqi, Kitab al-Buyu' & Bab kulli qardin jarra manfa'atan fa huwa riban)

From Anas ibn Malik (رضي الله عنه): The Prophet (صلى الله عليه وسلم), said: "If a man extends a loan to someone he should not accept a gift." (Mishkat, on the authority of Bukhara's Tarikh and Ibn Taymiyyah's al-Muntaqa)

From Abu Burdah ibn Abi Musa (رضي الله عنه): I came to Madinah and met 'Abdallah ibn Salam (رضي الله عنه) who said, "You live in a country where riba is rampant; hence, if anyone owes you something and presents you with a load of hay, or a load of barley, or a rope of straw, do not accept it for it is riba." (Mishkat reported on the authority of Bukhari)

Fadalah ibn 'Ubayd (رضي الله عنه) said that "The benefit derived from any loan is one of the different aspects of riba." (Sunan al-Bayhaqi) This hadith is mawquf implying that it is not necessarily from the Prophet (صلى الله عليه وسلم); it could be an explanation provided by Fadalah himself, a companion of the Prophet (صلى الله عليه وسلم).

Riba al Fadl

Riba of surplus or Riba al-Fadl comes into existence in a sale transaction that involves the exchange of one Ribawi commodity/Ribawi item (such as dates, wheat, etc.) for the same type of commodity but in different amount or weight. For example, the exchange of 10 kg of excellent-quality dates for 20 kg of poor quality dates.

The Prophet (ﷺ), said, "Sell gold in exchange of equivalent gold, sell silver in exchange of equivalent silver, sell dates in exchange of equivalent dates, sell wheat in exchange of equivalent wheat, sell salt in exchange for equivalent salt, sell barley in exchange of equivalent barley, but if a person transacts in excess, it will be usury (Riba). However, sell gold for silver anyway you please on the condition it is hand-to-hand (spot) and sell barley for a date besides you please on the condition it is hand-to-hand (spot)."

From Abu Sa'id al-Khudri (ﷺ): The Prophet (ﷺ), said: "Gold for gold, silver for silver, wheat for wheat, barley for barley, dates for dates, and salt for salt - like for like, and hand-to-hand. Whoever pays more or takes more has indulged in Riba. The taker and the giver are alike [in guilt]." (Muslim, ibid & Musnad Ahmad)

From Abu Sa'id: Bilal (ﷺ) brought to the Prophet (ﷺ), some Barni [good quality] dates whereupon the Prophet (ﷺ) asked him where these were from. Bilal replied, "I had some inferior dates which I exchanged for these - two sa's for a sa'." The Prophet (ﷺ) said, "Oh no, this is exactly Riba. Do not do so, but when you wish to buy, sell the inferior dates against something [cash] and then buy the better dates with the price you receive." (Muslim, Kitab al-Musaqat, Bab al-Ta'ami mithlan bi mithlin & Musnad Ahmad)

From Fadalah ibn 'Ubayd al-Ansari (ﷺ): On the day of Khaybar he bought a necklace of gold and pearls for twelve dinars. On separating the two, he found that the gold itself was equal to more than twelve dinars. So he mentioned this to the Prophet (ﷺ), who replied, "It [jewelry] must not be sold until the contents have been valued separately." (Muslim, Kitab al-Musaqat, Bab bay'i al-qiladah fiha khara-zun wa dhahab & in Tirmidhi and Nasa'i)

From Anas ibn Malik (ﷺ): The Prophet (ﷺ), said: "Deceiving a mustarsal [an unknowing entrant into the market] is riba." (Suyuti, al-Jami' al-Saghir, under the word ghabn; Kanz al-'Ummal, Kitab al-Buyu', al-Bab al-thani & al-fasl al-thani, on the authority of Sunan al-Bayhaqi)

From 'Abdallah ibn Abi Awfa (ﷺ): The Prophet (ﷺ), said: "A Najish [one who serves as an agent to bid up the price in an auction] is a cursed taker of riba." (Cited by Ibn Hajar al-'Asqalani in his commentary on al-Bukhari called Fath al-Bari, Kitab al-Buyu', Bab al-najsh; also in SuyutT, al-Jami al-Saghir, under the word al-najish and Kanz al-'Ummal, op. cit., both on the authority of Tabarani's al-Kabir).

CHAPTER – 16

TYPES OF RIBA

The word "Riba" means addition or expansion of something, Riba is translated by Shariah in the words, "Any addition/ excess payment without efforts." This meaning of Riba is extracted from the Holy Quran and is unanimously acknowledged by all Islamic researchers.

Types of Riba

There are two types of Riba: Riba-Al-Nasiyah and Riba-Al-Fadl.

a) Riba al Nasiah is the addition or increase demanded for delay in paying back the loan. It could be fixed prior to the transaction or on the occurrence of obligation. In such an event where the debtor is not ready to pay back the obligation on occurrence, the lender/ bank provides him extended time for an extra sum and it is termed Riba al Nasiah. The term Nasi'ah means to defer, concede or hold up to the time till the borrower is able to reimburse the credit with additional amount or the interest. Subsequently, Riba-al-Nasi'ah refers to the interest on loan. The term Riba appears in Qur'an in the verse "ALLAH(ﷻ) has forbidden interest" (2: 275). Maulana Mududi in his Tafheem ul Qur'an gives an explicit meaning of Riba al Nasi'ah while explaining the verse 275 of Surah Al Baqara, he writes:-

"At the time of the revelation of Qur'an, several forms of interest transactions were in vogue and were designated as Riba by the Arabs. Of these one was that the vendor sold an article and fixed a time limit for the payment of the price, stipulating that if the buyer failed to pay within the specified period of time, he would extend the time limit but increase the price of the article.

Another was that a man loaned a sum of money to another person and stipulated that the borrower should return a specified amount in excess of the amount loaned within a given time limit.

A third form of interest transaction was that the borrower and vendor agreed that the former would repay the loan within a certain limit at a fixed rate of interest and that if he failed to do so within the limit, the lender would extend the time limit, but at the same time would increase the rate of interest.

Qualities of Riba-Al-Nasiyah

Five characteristics of Riba al Nasiah are:-

i. It is altered (increases with the passage of time/ multiplies).

ii. It is ensured/ fixed.

iii. It secures the moneylender and exposes the borrower to an incredible risk.

vi. It is not allowed by ALLAH (ﷻ) and invites His indignation and fury.

b) Riba al-Fadl is not linked with delay or occurrence/ creation of obligation. It becomes payable when two quantities of the same thing are traded unequally. The Holy Qur'an had precluded the Riba of the dark era (Jahiliyya) or Riba al Nasiah with all its previous transactions and dues. All forms of Riba Al-Fadl linked with the transactions of a credit or an obligation made by the deal are also precluded. The Holy Prophet (ﷺ) felt that business environment in the Arab region and usual trade transactions/ business practices were likely to encourage people to indulge in Riba. Various types of business practices were declared unlawful because of their close link with Riba. For Riba Al-Fadl, the Arabs utilized certain things like wheat, grain, dates and so forth as a medium of trades, other than cash/ money. Any additional quantity given or received in exchange of same commodity is similar to giving or receiving additional cash. The Holy Prophet (ﷺ) clearly gave instruction for avoidance of such practices as given below:-

> "Gold for gold, silver for silver, wheat for wheat, barley for barley, date for the date, salt for the salt, must be equal on both sides and hand to hand. Whoever pays more or demands more (on either side) indulges in Riba."

It implies that if wheat is traded for wheat, the amount on both sides (receiving side and paying side) must be equivalent to one another and if there were unequally exchanged values, this transaction would be considered a Riba transaction. Consequently, it has been declared as "Riba al-Fadl".

CHAPTER – 17

SIMPLE AND COMPOUND INTEREST

An interest rate is a rate at which interest is paid by a borrower (account holder) for the utilization of cash obtained from a lender/ bank (loan provider). Interest rate is usually determined and fixed on yearly basis. Interest rates frequently change as a consequence of Federal Reserve Board strategies and policies.

Simple Interest

Simple interest is calculated on original principal amount only. Simple interest is ordinarily utilized for a short time less than a year, for example, 30 or 60 days. Interest is the expense of acquiring cash or the money obtained from lenders simply calculated once and the interest gained is not included in the principal amount for subsequent calculations.

Simple Interest = p * i * n

Where:

p = Principal amount (actual sum acquired or advance taken)

i = interest rate for one period

n = number of periods

Compound Interest

Compound interest is calculated for every period on the initial principal amount and all interest of past periods. Despite the fact that interest rate may be expressed as a yearly rate, the compounding periods might be on yearly, semi-annually, quarterly or even daily basis. Compound Interest implies that one gains "interest on one's interest payments as well". With Compound Interest, the interest is worked out for the first period, added it to the aggregate, and the interest for the next period is calculated, and so on.

$$A = P \left(1 + \frac{r}{n}\right)^{nt}$$

P = principal amount (the initial amount borrowed)

r = annual rate of interest (as a decimal)

t = number of years the amount is deposited or borrowed for.

A = amount of money accumulated after n years, including interest.

n = number of times interest is compounded per year

CHAPTER – 18

COMMERCIAL INTEREST & USUARY

Interest is an additional amount of money charged from the borrower for utilization of obtained loan/ cash/ advance.

Usury is a particular kind of investment that is not favorable for the borrower. While the capitalist law allows moneylenders to charge interest, loan providers cannot force borrowers to pay interest at usurious rates. The Holy Quran has strongly condemned the practice of promoting and adopting usury (Su'd or Riba) as a means of amassing unlawful money. As explained in the following verses of Holy Qur'an:-

> "ALLAH (ﷻ) has permitted Trade (commercial deal) and forbidden usury. Those who, after receiving Direction from their Lord, desist shall be forgiven for the past. Their case is for ALLAH (ﷻ) (to judge). But those who repeat (the offense) are companions of the Fire. They will abide therein forever. ALLAH (ﷻ) will deprive usury of all Blessing, but will give increase for deeds of charity. For He loveth not creatures (who are) ungrateful and wicked (Surah Baqara (2): Verse 275-276).

[Quran 3:130] O you who believe, you shall not take usury, compounded over and over. But fear ALLAH(ﷻ), that you may succeed.

[Quran 4:161] And for practicing usury, which was forbidden, and for consuming the people's money illicitly, We have prepared for the disbelievers among them painful retribution.

[Quran 30:39] The usury that is practiced to increase some people's wealth, does not gain anything from God. But if you give to charity, seeking God's pleasure, these are the ones who receive their reward manifold.

The Holy Prophet (ﷺ) has also condemned the dealing with usury in any manner.

"The man who accepts usury, who gives usury, one who writes the document on usury and those who stand witnesses to it, are all condemned as accursed."

He (ﷺ) has also said that:

"Though superficially the usury/interest gives an increase in the wealth but in consequence and in the longer run it cause diminution/decrease in one's assets".

When a business gets cash from a loan provider, the lender normally charges interest. However, there are certain regulations that a borrower must keep in view while making loan agreements and deciding about the interest rate to be paid. If the bank is found to be charging an interest higher than allowed by regulations, the bank is practicing Usury.

Without Riba, an economy will look drastically unique in relation to an economy focused on interest-based loans, so this difference has great impact on the government, regional culture and organizations.

Contemplations

Prior to the formation of usury laws, the expression "usury" was basically an alternate word for interest. National banks and government sponsored reserve funds/ banks are excluded from usury laws. However, they should not charge interest rates more than the laid down rates by Federal Reserve Banks/ National Banks.

SECTION – 06

ISLAMIC INVESTMENT

Islamic financial institutions, particularly in Islamic countries offer different types of investment products that are free of Riba or premium. An Islamic financing deposit is generally one type of investment in which various individuals pool their cash and the same is put into a legitimate Islamic way/ business. The expression "Islamic Investment Fund" implies a joint pool wherein the investors invest their surplus cash to obtain Halaal (permissible) benefits in strict compliance with the laws of Shariah.

CHAPTER – 19

ISLAMIC INVESTMENT FUNDS

The 'Islamic Investment Fund' is a joint pool in which the investors deposit their surplus cash with the sole aim of investing in Islamic businesses. Benefits are likewise reaped from the profits appropriated by pertinent business organizations doing business with the said investment.

Favorable Circumstances

These Investment Funds have clear focal responsibility to Muslims, who can invest their cash knowing that the Investment Fund will not go against any of their religious convictions. Numerous Investment Funds have been around for quite a while and have a decent track record of creating solid returns for their investors.

Difficulties

Since Islamic principles prohibit the utilization of interest-paying instruments, the Islamic Investment Funds do not invest money in such instruments.

The vast majority of the investment institutions aim to attract big investors, large corporations and multinational companies instead of small investors. In Islamic Investment Funds most of the investment comes from small investors. Deposits range from the US $50,000 to as high as US $1 million.

Investment Checklist

First point on the check list for an investor who wants to invest in an Islamic Investment Fund is a warning. He/ she should only consider putting resources into Islamic Investment Funds after accepting the hazard that he/ she may experience loss from your invested principal amount. Remaining points, whatsoever, are similar to all other non-Islamic investments.

Some Thumb Rules for Investment

Do's

Analyze investment in Islamic Investment Funds on the same lines as you would have analyzed other investment options. Clearly visualize whether you want to earn a big amount of profit or would be satisfied with small gains, similarly make a decision for tying up your money for a long period. Most of the experts agree that through such type of investment a handsome gain will only be possible if the investment period is not less than five years. Other options of investment have their own hazards like individuals should be aware of the danger of putting resources into stocks that may go down.

Don'ts

Don't contribute without investigating the large variety of Investment Fund available to investors, which is best suited to your needs.

Don't contribute without expert advice from any financial advisor. Verify that they don't acquire any commission for proposing customers to a certain fund.

CHAPTER – 20

STOCKS AND SECURITIES (SECURITIZATION)

Introduction of Stocks and Securities

While describing securities, emphasis is usually on the techniques – the methodology of pooling assets, the procedure of packaging them into securities and the procedure of issuing securities to financial institutions/ public. Given the Islamic basis of a business to be interest free, for acceptance of the stocks and securities business as an Islamic investment, focus has to be on substance of the "package" rather than methodology of packaging. Consequently, they have a tendency to guarantee that the benefits in the package – and not the package itself – are 'Islamically acceptable' (interest free). In reality, the package as well as its benefits, all have to be essentially interest free.

Securitization or Taskeek in Arabic refers to the process of division of ownership of tangible assets or rights to use those assets, and assigning them to units which have equal value for issuance to investors. In simple terms, securitization is the process of aggregating assets and packaging them into marketable securities.

Types of Securities

1. Receivable Securitization (Debt Securitization).
2. Asset-based/ project-based/ ownership-based/ use-based securitization.
3. Asset-backed securities i.e. Securities backed by established income stream prior to securitization.

CHAPTER – 21

THE PRINCIPLE OF LIMITED LIABILITY

Rasulullah (ﷺ) once said:-

> "The truthful and honest trader will be (on the Day of Qiyaamah) with the Ambiya, the Siddiqeen and the Shuhada (Martyrs)."

Limited liability is considered as a "foundation" of the Islamic business laws and quite suitable for newly established organizations whose partners are not sure of the success of organization. The idea of limited liability is critical to the viable working of organizations.

In a limited liability organization, the risk does not exceed the total sum of the value of original resources. The limited liability characteristic is one of the most favorable conditions for putting resources at risk in vulnerable organizations. While a shareholder is involved and desires development of an organization, his or her risk is confined to the amount of venture/ investment in the organization, immune to the possibility of personal liability or bankruptcy.

Discussion

The concept of 'limited liability' has now become an inseparable ingredient of the large-scale enterprises of trade and industry throughout the modern world, including Muslim countries. This chapter aims to explain this concept and evaluate it from the Shari'ah point of view in order to know whether or not this principle is acceptable in a pure Islamic economy. The concept of limited liability' in modern economics and legal terminology is a condition under which a partner or a shareholder of a business secures himself from bearing a loss greater than the amount he has invested in a company or partnership with limited liability. If the business incurs a loss, the maximum liability a shareholder must face is that he may lose his entire original investment. But the loss cannot extend to his personal assets and if the assets of the company are not sufficient to discharge all its liabilities, the creditors cannot claim the remaining part of their receivables from the personal assets of the shareholders.

Although the concept of 'limited liability' was, in some countries applied to the partnership also, yet, it was most commonly applied to companies and corporate bodies. Rather, historically, to say that the concept of 'limited liability' originally emerged with the emergence of the corporate bodies and joint stock companies. The basic purpose of the introduction of this principle was to attract maximum number of investors to the large-scale joint ventures and to assure them that their personal fortunes will not be at stake if they wish to invest their savings in such a joint enterprise. In practice of modern trade, the concept proved itself to be a vital force to mobilize large amounts of capital from a wide range of investors.

There is no doubt that the concept of limited liability is beneficial to the shareholders of a company. But, at the same time, it may be injurious to its creditors. If the liabilities of a limited company exceed its assets, the company becomes insolvent and it is consequently liquidated. In this scenario, the creditors may lose a considerable amount of their claims because they can only receive the liquidated value of the company's asset and have no recourse to its shareholders for the rest of their claims. Even the directors of the company who may be responsible for such an unfortunate situation cannot be held responsible for creditor's claim. It is this aspect of the concept of 'limited liability' which requires consideration and research from the Shari'ah viewpoint.

SECTION - 07

ASSET-BACKED FINANCING

It is the act of taking a loan/ advance on the guarantee of an asset. Similarly, as with all secured loans, asset-backed credits have lower interest rates than unsecured credits. The practice is additionally called asset-backed financing.

It is a secured business loan in which the borrower vows as guarantee any assets of his/ her business. Additionally, it is called business loan or asset based lending.

It is a particular technique for providing working capital and term credits that are secured by accounts receivable, inventory, supplies and/ or land/ fixed assets. Asset-backed finance helps businesses take advantage of opportunities in construction, transport, manufacturing/ processing, mining/ quarrying, printing and material handling.

CHAPTER – 22

IJARA

It is a sort of an agreement in Islamic finance. "Ijarah" is a term of Islamic Fiqh, lexically, it signifies 'to give something on rent'. Ijara is a trade transaction in which a known profit emerging from an asset is gained as an exchange for allowing temporary use or possession, however, ownership itself is not exchanged.

Kinds of Ijarah

In the Islamic law, the expression "Ijarah" is utilized for two distinct conditions. In one case, it signifies 'to utilize the services of an individual' on wages given to him as a compensation for his contracted services. The manager is called "Mustajir" while the principal is called 'Ajir' while the wages paid to the Ajir are called 'Ujrah'.

The second kind of Ijarah is utilization of assets and properties for a rent. "Ijarah" in this sense implies "to exchange the right to use a specific property with someone else in return for a rent guaranteed from him". In this case, the expression "Ijarah" is practically equivalent to the English term 'renting'. Here the owner of property who rents it is called 'Mujir', the person taking an asset on rent is called "Mustajir" and the rent payable to the person is called 'Ujrah'.

Practical Application of Ijarah

The principles of Ijarah are comparable to a lease agreement, in both cases something is exchanged for something. The main distinction between Ijarah and lease is that in lease the legal ownership of the property is exchanged, while on account of Ijarah, the legal ownership of the property stays with the owner while the right to utilize it, is given to the tenant.

No rental will be expected if the rentor/ lessor fails to transfer the asset to the tenant on the date fixed in the Ijarah contract. At the completion of the Ijarah contract, the renter has one of three alternatives; either to return asset to the lessor or to make lease contract for another term or to buy the rented asset at a cost determined by the asset owner.

Ijarah income (when the Islamic bank is a lessor) and cost (when the Islamic bank is a tenant) are perceived when the Ijarah rent gets due. Ordinarily, the lessor is responsible for major repairs (other than occasional ones; which are borne by the tenant) unless they are the aftereffect of the resident's abuse or damage. The Islamic bank ought to declare the bookkeeping strategies used for working out Ijarah and Ijara Muntahia Bittamleek in the notes appearing in the bank's money related documents and annual reports.

Conditions of Ijarah

Some of the most usually occurring conditions for Ijara to be valid are as under:-

    a) The rented commodity should be in working condition.

    b) The rented asset ought to be tangible.

c) The amount of money and timings of the rent/ lease installments ought to be decided beforehand, however, the agreed time periods and amount of installments may not be uniform.

d) The rent/ lease installments become due upon complete possession of the asset, whether such asset is utilized by the lessor or not.

e) The time of the rent/ lease must be clearly defined.

f) The physical state of use of the rented asset must be expressed so that damage, if any, can be assessed at the end of rent/ lease contract.

g) The rentor/ lessor must have full ownership and lawful possession before renting an asset to someone.

h) The rented asset must exist throughout the term of the rent/ lease.

i) Conversely, with most traditional rents contracts, the obligation regarding upkeep and protection of the rented property/ asset under ijara remains that of the lessor's responsibility throughout the rent/ lease term.

CHAPTER – 23

ISTISNA'A SALE

Istisna'a is an offer in which an item is sold before its production. It is a request in which a producer/ manufacturer to produce a particular item/ product for the buyer. The agreement of Istisna'a ensures an ethical commitment by the producer to make the product, yet before he begins the work, any of the parties may terminate the agreement by giving a notice to the other. However, after the producer has begun work of production/ manufacture, the agreement cannot be terminated unilaterally.

Istisna'a is a Sharia mode of financing broadly used by Islamic banks and financial organizations to fund the development of buildings/ constructions, assembling of airplanes, ships, machines, and so forth. The Arabic word "Istisna'a" signifies "requesting somebody to produce". It may be further described and explained as a contract between the manufacturer and the purchaser for producing an asset according to the contract prior to manufacturing the asset/ product.

Terms of Istisna'a Agreement/ Contract
- Terms of Financing.
- Type of asset/ product to be produced and its specifications.

- Money Contribution: Minimum 40% to half of aggregate venture cost.
- Fund Tenure: 10 years including up to two years development period.
- Mode of Payment: Monthly, Quarterly, Semi-yearly or Annual terms.
- Means of Payment; Primary: Rental pay of the task. Optional: Other livelihoods.
- Profit Rate: Fixed throughout the financing period.
- Security: First degree enlisted home loan on the plot and the building, notwithstanding alternate terms of endorsement.
- Protection: Insurance arrangement covering the property under development to be relegated to the Bank.
- Qualified Assets: Residential, Office Buildings & Villa Complexes.
- Documentary Requirements.
- Next of Kin in case of death of contracting individuals.
- Complete payment record and schedule.
- Final payment end state.
- Feasibility Study ready by hired advisor.
- Venture detail and affirmed drawings.
- Copy of the expert/ builder agreement.

Procedure of Istisna'a Sale

- The procedure begins when a client communicates the dealer his intention to buy a product that must be produced, fabricated or gathered with specifications and detailed cost.
- The dealer and the client enter into an Istisna'a contract under which the dealer agrees to have the product fabricated and conveyed to the client within a certain period of time at a given cost payable on the

spot or by regular installments or in lump sum on agreed terms.

- The dealer then enters into an Istisna'a contract with manufacturer to produce the product.

Parties of Istisna'a Contract

- Istisna'a requester: is the purchaser (manager of the task).
- Dealer: who enters into a contract with the Istisna'a requester and promises to provide the product. He also enters into contract with producer.
- Product Manufacturer: is the producer of the product who is under agreement with the dealer.

Essential Details for Istisna'a Contract

- The product must be specified as clearly as possible including following details:
  - Product details (vehicle, land, and so forth).
  - Type (brand and make).
  - Description (specifications/ requirements to be fulfilled).
- Permitted Deferment
  - The subject item is to be produced or procured from other business sectors. In this manner, a delivery/ provision date must be defined with a specific end state.
  - The period of delivery/ provision depends upon the agreement of the two parties which must be clearly mentioned in the contract.
- Price
  - The cost is to be explicitly mentioned in the contract and must be known to the two parties.
  - The value may be balanced if alterations are made to the contracted item by the shared assertion of the two parties.

CHAPTER – 24

MURABAHA SALE

Introduction of Murabaha

Murabaha is not an interest-bearing credit or loan which can be considered Riba (or over abundance/ compound interest). Murabaha is an acceptable type of credit or loan under Shariah (Islamic law). Murabaha is consistent with Shariah, where the dealer explicitly specifies the expense he has made on the product available to be sold and offers it to someone else by including some benefit or profit subsequently which is known to the purchaser.

The Bai' Murabaha includes buying of product by a dealer for selling it to customers on some profit which is known to the customer. Under this contract/ method, the dealer unveils his cost and net profit to the customer before the contract. The dealer purchases the products from merchant/ manufacturer and offer that product to the client at an agreed cost.

Uses of Murabaha

It is one of the most common mainstream modes of business utilized by banks/ dealers in Islamic nations. Several banks utilize this instrument with changing proportions. Normally, banks use Murabaha in asset financing, property, and microfinance. Large number of Islamic banks and financial institutions are using

Murabaha as an Islamic mode of financing, and a greater part of their financing operations are focused around Murabaha.

Essential Rules for Murabaha

- The product/ asset/ subject of offer must exist at the time of the deal. In this manner, anything that does not exist at the time of offer cannot be sold, as this makes the agreement void.
- The product/ asset/ subject ought to be in the possession of the dealer at the time of the offer. In case, the vender offers something that he himself has not procured, the deal gets void.
- The product/ asset/ subject of an offer must be in physical or productive ownership of the vender when it is sold to another person.
- The deal must be instant and best. In this way a deal credited to a future date or a deal dependent upon a future occasion is void.
- The product/ asset/ subject ought to be a property having approval according to Shari'ah.
- The product/ asset/ subject of an offer ought not to be an instrument utilized for an un-Islamic reason.
- The product/ asset/ subject of an offer must be particularly known and distinguished to the purchaser.
- The conveyance of the sold item to the purchaser must be sure and ought not to rely upon a possibility.
- The cost is an essential condition for the legitimacy of the deal. In case the cost is unverifiable, the deal is void.
- The deal must be unconditional. A contingent deal is invalid unless the condition is perceived as a piece of the transaction as per the utilization of the exchange.

Issues in Murabaha

Securities against Murabaha

Installments originating from the deal are receivables and for this, the customer may be asked to provide a security.

Guaranteeing the Murabaha

The dealer can ask the customer to provide a third party assurance. In case of default on payment of installments, the producer may have to inform the underwriter who will have to pay the sum on behalf of the customer.

Punishment for Default

An alternate issue with Murabaha is that if the customer defaults in payment of installments on the due date, the cost cannot be changed nor some additional money can be charged as fine.

To deal with exploitative customers who default in the installment deliberately, they ought to be made to pay Islamic Bank for loss occurred because of default. However, these ought to be done in following conditions:-

- The defaulter may be given a grace period of minimum one month.
- If default is without substantial reasons, repayment might be demanded.

Rollover in Murabaha

Murabaha transaction cannot be moved over for a further period as the old contract closes. It must to be comprehended that Murabaha is not a loan rather offering a product/ item which is conceded to a particular date. When the product is sold, its possession exchanges from the bank/ dealer to the customer and it is accordingly no more a property of the producer or dealer. The dealer can only claim the concurred cost and there is no chance of affecting an alternate deal on the same item between same parties.

Refund on Prior Installments

At times, the indebted individuals need to pay right on time to get rebates. However, in Islam, majority of Muslim Scholars including the factual schools of thought consider this to be un–Islamic.

CHAPTER – 25

SALAM SALE

Introduction of Salam

Salam is a loan financing transaction, where the financial institution pays ahead of time for purchasing the desired asset, which the dealer has to supply on specific date. In return for the advance payment of cost should not be in the form of cash, otherwise, it will be Riba by definition. As a return for payment ahead of time, contracting parties stipulate a future date for the supply of product at concurred price.

Salam may be considered as a sort of obligation/ liability, the dealer has to face risk equal to the cost of the product till concurred future date to deliver the item for which advance payment of the cost has been made. There is consensus among Muslim law specialists on the reasonability of Salam, despite the general principle of Shari'ah that does not allow offering an item which is not in ownership of the merchant, on the grounds that the objective of the agreement is facilitation of the buyer and seller, it is allowed.

However, Salam cannot occur between indistinguishable products. Moreover, the time and place of conveyance of the product ought to be exactly decided and quality and price of the products ought to be obviously known. The most crucial condition of Salam is to pay the cost to the seller at time of the agreement.

Validation of Salam

The validity of this sale is evidenced by a narration on the authority of Ibn 'Abbaas (رضي الله عنه) and his father that the Prophet (ﷺ), came to Medina and the people used to pay in advance the price of fruits to be delivered within two to three years. He (ﷺ), said (to them),

> "Whoever pays in advance should do this for a fixed specified measure, specified weight, and a specified [delivery] period." [Al-Bukhaari & Muslim]

It is also narrated on the authority of 'Abdur-Rahmaan ibn Abza and 'Abdullaah ibn Abi Awfa (رضي الله عنه) who have said,

> "We used to get war booty while we were with the Messenger of ALLAH (ﷺ), and when the peasants of Ash-Shaam came to us we used to pay them in advance for wheat, barley, and oil to be delivered within a fixed period." They were asked, "Did the peasants own standing crops or not?" They replied, "We never asked them about it." [Al-Bukhaari]

Applicability of Salam

Bai-Salam has been allowed by the Holy Prophet (ﷺ) himself, without any difference of opinion among the early or contemporary legal advisers, despite the general rule of Shariah that the offer of a product which is not in the ownership of the dealer is not allowed. Upon movement from Makkah, the Prophet (ﷺ) came to Medina, where the individuals used to pay ahead of time the cost of tree-grown foods or dates to be conveyed in advance of one or few years. On the other hands, such deal was completed without defining the quality, measurement or weight of the product or the time of conveyance. The Prophet (ﷺ) said:

> "Whoever pays cash ahead of time for soil grown foods to be conveyed later ought to pay it for a known quality, defined measure and weight (of dates or apples and oranges) obviously alongside the value and time of conveyance."

Conditions in Salam

The Salam transaction is liable to strict conditions for being valid as follows:-

- It is important for the legitimacy of Salam that the purchaser decides over the required money from the dealer at the time of deal. Without full payment, it will be equivalent to offer of an obligation against an obligation, which is explicitly restricted by the Holy Prophet (ﷺ).
- Only those products could be sold through a Salam contract in which the amount and quality might be precisely determined e.g. valuable stones cannot be sold on the contract of Salam as each one is different in quality, size, weight and their definite price is impossible to determine.
- Salam cannot be used on non-specific item or on a result of a specific item e.g. fruit of a specific tree.
- All relevant points about the kind and nature of product must be explicitly pointed out leaving no ambiguity.
- It is vital that the cost of the product is agreed upon in exact terms.
- The definite date and place of conveyance must be given in the agreement.

- Salam cannot be used for things which are delivered on spot.
- The period of delivery ought to be not less than fifteen days or one month from the date of agreement. The cost of Salam is, by and large, lower than the spot price.

The Individuals included in a Salam Transaction

- Customer – Rabbul-mal
- Retailer-Muslam ilayh
- Capital (money paid) – Ra'sul-mal
- Item – Muslam fih

Motivation behind Utilization

To meet the need of low income farmers who need cash to prepare their fields and to support their family till the time of harvest, Salam is allowed. ALLAH (ﷻ) proclaimed interest as impermissible, the farmers could not take usurious loans. Thus, the Prophet (ﷺ) permitted them to offer their agricultural products ahead of time. Salam was useful to the seller because he used to get the cost ahead of time and it was advantageous to the purchaser because typically the cost of Salam used to be lower than the cost of spot deals.

The Conditions for Salam

Salam must be used in things that can be weighed, measured or in things comprising units that are sold by units. Accordingly, Salam will be useful to deal with crops, for example, wheat, grain, dates and so on. Salam is not be allowed in live-stocks. The requested thing must be specified in quantity and quality in every conceivable way:-

a) The obtained thing must be desired.
b) The quality must be laid down.
c) The procurement of the things must be desired.
d) The cost must be decided.
e) The time of the conveyance must be decided.

Risk Management in Salam

Islamic banks need to take special care in Salam operations. They face a number of risks.

- **Third-party Risk** is one of the common risks in Salam-based financing, in fact, the client may default after taking the money in advance.
- **Commodity Price Risk**, at the time goods are received, the price may be lower than the price that was originally expected, it is another risk associated to Salam.
- There is also **Quality Risk**, low investment Return or Loss, which occurs when goods received are not of desired quality or unacceptable for the potential buyer.
- In case the Islamic bank has to purchase goods from the market in parallel Salam, where the third party fails to supply the specified goods under the parallel contract, the bank faces an **Asset-Replacement Risk**.
- Finally, in parallel Salam, if the original Salam seller has not delivered the goods as expected, it is considered as **Fiduciary Risk**.

In order to manage and mitigate the above risks, Islamic banks need to take proper measures. In fact, Islamic banks purchase only goods that have good marketing potential; they take proper security and a performance bond; they require from the prospective buyers a sufficient amount of earnest money in deposit and a binding promise to purchase these goods; they also insert a penalty clause in the Salam contract to protect themselves from a late delivery from the supplier; and they accomplish the responsibility of parallel Salam by purchasing similar goods from the market on spot to supply these to the buyer and recover the loss, if any, from the seller in the original Salam.

SECTION - 08

ISLAMIC MODES OF FINANCING

The methods of Islamic finance are following:

- Ijarah (Leasing/A rental agreement)
- Ijarah-wa-Iqtina
- Bai Salam (Spot payment for future delivery)
- Istisnaa (Order to manufacturer)
- Murabaha (Cost plus profit sale)
- Istijrar
- Musharaka
- Diminishing Musharaka (House financing)
- Modaraba
- Bai Muajjal (Credit sale)
- Musawama
- Hiba
- Wakalah (Power of attorney)
- Wadiah (Safe keeping)
- Takaful (Islamic insurance)
- Sukuk (Islamic bonds)
- Qard Hassan (Good loan)

CHAPTER – 26

IJARAH (LEASING/A RENTAL AGREEMENT)

Ijarah is a transfer transaction prevalent in the Islamic regions. This is analogous to a kind of mortgage loan with no requirement for down-payment. It is mainly a word of Islamic Fiqh, lexically, it indicates 'to offer something on payment/ rent'. In the jurisprudence of Islam, this term can be used for two diverse conditions. In the first condition, it generally means 'to use the services of someone on salary/ wages specified to him as a compensation for his services. The individual asking for services/ boss is known as 'Musta'jir' while the worker/ employee is known as 'Ajir'. The second condition entails hiring assets and properties, does not refer to the services of people. It means, to temporarily give an asset/ property to another person in exchange for a rental fee. In this sense, this term is similar to the English word 'leasing'. Here the lessor is known to be as 'Mu'ajir', the renter is known to be as 'Musta'jir' and the payable rent to the lessor is known as 'Ujrah'.

Validation of Ijarah

Some legal experts describe Ijarah as the right to use an asset/ property for a certain time period in return for rent. For validity of Ijarah, the asset must be rented/ leased by the renter/ organization. It is a binding agreement/ contract which neither of the parties can terminate or change without the other party's permission.

No payment will be payable if the lessor fails to provide the asset to lessee on the date expressed in Ijarah. At the end of the contract the occupant has one of three alternatives; to return the leased asset to the lessor or to renew the lease agreement for another term or to acquire the leased asset for a price that is determined based on lease payments decided by the renter.

Ijarah proceeds and expenditures are separated when the Ijarah installment becomes payable. As a rule, the owner will be accountable for main repairs/ renovations except the damages or unfair wear and tear done by lessee for which he will pay for restoration of property to its original condition. The Islamic financial institutions should formulate the accounting rules for using such type of contracts.

CHAPTER – 27

IJARAH WA IQTINA

Under this agreement, an Islamic financial institution acquires an asset, for instance equipment, vehicles or buildings for giving on lease to a customer for rental payments. The ownership rights are shifted to the lessee at the end of contract. It is also known as Ijarah Muntahia-bi-tamleek.

The Essentials of Ijara-Wa-Iqtina

The process of Ijara-Wa-Iqtina starts with a client approaching a financial institution by means of a request to get the desired asset on lease. With this in view, the financial institution purchases the asset and gives it on lease to the client under a lease agreement. Time period and rental payments are decided. The right of possession of the asset remains with the lessor and right of use is given to the client/ lessee. The lessee makes the first rental payment on the day he takes delivery of the asset or the right to utilize the asset specified in the agreement. This type of contract is not much different from other forms of ijara agreements except at the end of contract/ agreement the ownership right is shifted from the financial institution/ lessor to lessee.

Conversely, on this occasion, it should be made obvious that the soundness of such type of agreement rests on these three conditions:

• The lease and the shifting of ownership of the asset should be guaranteed in contracts.

• The leasing and the shifting of ownership agreements should be autonomous of each other. In additional terms, the "guarantee" of a shifting of rights should not be a prerequisite to the signing of the leasing agreement.

• The "guarantee" to shift the rights should be one-sided and should be compulsory just on the lessor.

Benefits of Ijara wa Iqtina

The extensive occurrence of Ijara wa Iqtina is simple to appreciate if you think the countless benefits of this style of Islamic financial agreements. Here are a few of the benefits:-

• It permits business proprietors of various sizes to enjoy the benefits of using a good or an asset without purchasing it. This is particularly suitable for cash deficient business proprietors who do not have the money to acquire a portion of equipment or apparatus for manufacturing/ production.

• The exact features of this agreement are particularly suitable for business proprietors who currently have the need for an additional equipment/ asset but do not desire to purchase it because of its low resale/ residual price.

• The option of being able to transfer the rights of an asset is also advantageous for the lessor, because he is not burdened with liability of owning the asset at the end of lease period.

The simplicity and transparency of dealings and benefits for both lessor and the lessee are the causes for preference of salam agreements.

CHAPTER – 28

BAI SALAM

It is a deal whereby the vendor promises to provide an asset to the purchaser at a future date in an exchange of cost totally paid in advance. At this point, the cost is paid in cash like normal on spot sale, except the delivery of the asset is delayed till a specific time. The consumer is known as "Rabb-us-Salam", the vendor is "Muslam Ilaih", the cash value is "Ra's-ul-Mal" and the procured product is known as "Muslam Fih.

Salam was permitted by the Holy Prophet (ﷺ) subject conditions which have to be certain/ stable. The philosophy behind this transaction was to meet the requirements of the small farmers who required cash to prepare their fields for crops and to meet their household expenses up to the time of yield. Subsequent to the ban of Riba, they could not get usurious loans. As a result, it was permitted for them to sell their crops in advance before harvest.

It was helpful for the farmer as he received the cost in advance, and it was useful for the purchaser because the cost of Salam was inferior to the spot price of the good/ asset. In Islamic financing, it is basically an agreement for the purchase of commodities to be made available at a particular moment in the future. Payment for the commodities is made in advance.

It is an agreement in which advance payment is paid for products to be carried at a future date, in accordance with Islam and Islamic Shariah. The supplier promises to provide a quantity of definite products to the purchaser at a future date in exchange for an advance cost completely paid at the time of agreement. It is essential that quality of product to be acquired is clearly laid down leaving no ambiguity to either of the parties. For Islamic financial institutions, this operation is a best way for agricultural financing. It is one of the preferred Islamic modes of finance used by financial institutions in Islamic countries to encourage Riba-free dealings.

CHAPTER – 29

ISTISNA'A (ORDER TO MANUFACTURE)

The Arabic term "Istisna'a" denotes "requesting a producer to manufacture". It is, in general, an agreement for producing an item in which the company agrees to produce a particular item as per given specifications to be delivered at a specific time, place and cost.

Application of Istisna'a

It is extensively used by Islamic financial institutions for the purpose of construction of buildings, residential towers and other associated entities as well as manufacturing of aircrafts, ships, machines and equipment, etc. It is basically an agreement wherein a buyer procures an item with delayed delivery. The product must be specified in detail and has to meet all the given requirements. There is no standard release time for the product and this agreement is made for custom-ordered products.

Principles of Istisna'a

There are some basic principles of Istisna'a, which are as follows:-

- The characteristics and specifications of the item to be produced have to be specified.
- The producer has to make a promise to manufacture the good as specified.

- The release date is not to be fixed.
- The agreement is binding subsequent to the beginning of production apart from where the item does not meet the specifications.
- Payment may be completed at one time or in installments over a period of time till the time of delivery/ release.
- The producer is responsible for the sourcing of materials and labors to the manufacturing factory/ place.

   In this agreement, the cost has to be predetermined by consensus of all concerned. All supplementary requirements of the product are to be wholly specified.

Annulment of Agreement

Subsequent to giving early notice, one can terminate the agreement before the job has begun. Once the job begins, the agreement cannot be terminated unilaterally.

Istisna'a as a Mode of Financing

It is mostly used to offer loan for housing finance. If the customer owns a piece of land and searches for finance for building a house, he possibly will assume to build the house through Istisna'a. If the customer does not own land and desires to buy that also, the bank/ financial institution can still construct a house on a particular piece of the land for the client. The investment bank is not obliged to build the house itself and can enter into an equivalent Istisna'a with any third party or employ a service provider. He has to control the cost of Istisna'a for earning reasonable profit. The imbursement of payments by the customer may begin right on the day of agreement of Istisna'a. The bank/ financial institution is responsible for building the house as per given specifications in the agreement. The cost of correcting any inconsistency would be borne by investment institution.

CHAPTER – 30

MURABAHA (COST PLUS PROFIT SALE)

Introduction of Murabaha

This type of transaction is compatible with the laws of Shariah. The vendor presents his product in the market and tells characteristics of the product, then he fixes a price which comprises cost of the product and his profit and finally negotiates with the buyers. It is an Islamic financing mode, where an intermediary buys a property with free and clear title to it. The intermediary and the prospective buyer then agree upon a sale price (including an agreed upon profit for the intermediary) that can be made through a series of installments, or as a lump sum payment. Murabaha is not an interest-bearing loan, which is considered Riba (or excess). Murabaha is an acceptable form of credit sale under Sharia (Islamic religious law).

Murabaha is a particular kind of sale where the seller explicitly mentions the cost of the sold commodity he has incurred and sells it to another person by adding some profit thereon. Thus, Murabaha is not a loan given on interest; it is a sale of a commodity for cash/ deferred price. The Bai' Murabaha involves the purchase of a commodity by a bank on behalf of a client and its resale to the latter on the cost-plus-profit basis. Under this arrangement, the bank discloses its cost and profit margin to the client. In other words rather than lending money to a borrower like in a conventional banking agreement, the bank will buy the goods from a third party and sell those goods on to the customer for a pre-agreed price. Murabaha is a mode of financing as old as Musharaka. Today over 66% of all investment transactions are through Murabaha in Islamic banks.

Application of Murabaha

This mode is used by financial institutions in Islamic states to endorse Riba-free businesses. Various financial institutions use this tool in anecdotal relations. Financial institutions use Murabaha in asset financing, possessions, microfinance and product import-export. The book-keeping action of Murabaha, and its revelation and appearance in monetary declarations differ from bank to bank. Murabaha is a Shariah compliant financing method, with which you can buy a local commodity, owned by the bank. Under the Murabaha Loan Financing technique, the bank buys and owns the commodities requested by the customer, and then sell to the customer on installment at a prefixed profit margin.

Difference between Murabaha and Sale

A simple sale in Arabic is called Musawama - a bargaining sale without disclosing or referring to what the cost price is. However, when the cost price is disclosed to the client it is called Murabaha. A simple Murabaha is one where there is cash payment and Murabaha Muajjal is one on deferred payment basis.

Uses of Murabaha

Murabaha can be used in following conditions:-

- Short/Medium/Long Term Financing for:-

- o Raw material
- o Inventory
- o Equipment
- o Asset financing
- o Import financing
- o Export financing (Pre-shipment)
- o Consumer goods financing
- o House financing
- o Vehicle financing
- o Land financing
- o Tour package financing
- o Education package financing
- All other services that can be sold in the form of package (i.e. services like education, medical, etc.).

CHAPTER – 31

ISTIJRAR

Introduction of Istijrar

The expression "Bai-Istijrar" has been taken from Arabic words بیع(Bai) and جر(Zarra). The term Bai means to buy/ offer and Zarra means to pick up/ get/ raise. "Istijrar" (استجرار) means to buy goods/ assets occasionally in differing quantities. In Islamic law "Istijrar" is an assertion where a purchaser buys something under a solitary understanding in diverse quantities. However, no offer and acknowledgement is necessary at the occasion of deal. This arrangement will be considered as a solitary understanding where all terms and conditions are finalized. "Bai-Istijrar" is like sale/ purchase where an individual continues taking a delivery of items from a supplier and no offer (Ijaab) and acknowledgment (Qubul) and bartering between them occurs at every time of sale/ purchase.

It is like an agreement between a customer and a supplier, where the supplier consents to deliver a product/ asset at a future time, at an agreed cost and mode of payment.

Types of Istijrar

There are two sorts of Istijrar:

- A type whereby the price is already decided and delivery of products/ assets continues periodically. There is no requirement for negotiating price for each transaction. Payment of price/ Cost is done at the end. For example an inventory manager receives raw material from a vendor.
- A sort whereby the price is required to be negotiated for each transaction. For example a customer orders a vehicle.

It is in consonance with Islamic mode of financing. This kind is permissible with certain conditions as given below:-

- In the case where the dealer reveals the actual cost of goods at the time of each deal, the sale becomes lawful. The amount is paid after all dealings have been finalized.
- If the seller/ dealer does not reveal every time the actual cost of the goods, but purchaser knows that it is being sold on market value and the market value is specified and determined in such a manner that it does not vary and it does not lead to price differences for the purchasers.
- If at the time of ownership, the price of goods was unknown or buyers agree that whatever the price shall be, the sale will be executed. However, if there is a significant difference in the market price and the agreed price, it may cause conflict. In such a case, at the time of possession, the sale will not be valid. However, at the time of settlement of the payment, the sale will be valid.

CHAPTER – 32

MUSHARAKA

Introduction of Musharaka

"Musharaka" is a term of the Arabic language which means sharing. In business and exchange, it implies a joint endeavor in which all the participants share the profit or loss of the joint venture. Musharaka (Organization/ Partnership) is one of the financing contracts utilized by Islamic banks. A Musharaka contract is an assertion where two or more parties (for instance an Islamic bank and its customers) agree to contribute capital, in a trade or in a kind of business, no obligation to share the capital equally which can also be done equally or in differing proportions.

Importance of Musharaka

The exact meaning of Musharaka is sharing and source of the word "Musharaka" in Arabic is Shirkah, which means being a partner. Under Islamic law, Musharaka implies a joint endeavor framed for a businesses in which all participants share the profit as indicated by a particular proportion while the loss is shared as per the degree of the commitment/ investment.

Application of Musharaka

It is essentially an organization comprising two or more parties including a general blend of capital and abilities under an agreement. It is a joint venture or association with profit/ loss sharing ramifications that are utilized by Islamic banks rather than interest bearing credits. Musharaka permits the sharing of risk and returns as opposed to charging interest from a borrower, the beneficiary will get a return as a part of the genuine profit earned according to a pre-determined ratio. However, contrary to a customary loan provider, the beneficiary will also bear the potential risk of losses. Musharaka assumes an indispensable part in financing business focused on Islamic laws which forbid interest on loan.

The extent of benefit to be appropriated between the participants must be agreed upon at the time of negotiations/ agreement. If the extent or ratio of profit sharing is not explicitly laid down, the agreement is not legitimate in Shari'ah.

The Application of Musharaka in Diverse Types of Financing

Application of Musharaka in Local Trade

An obvious application is in local trade where the bank enters into an agreement with the customer. A separate Musharaka record is opened at the bank promptly after signing of the agreement, which contains all transactions relating to this record. It is the obligation of the participants to plan sale/ execute activities to earn profits.

Application of Musharaka to the Import of Merchandise

The shipper asks the bank to arrange import and offer specific products in the local markets. The aggregate expense of importing the products is shared between the bank and other participants of agreement.

Letters of Credit (LOC) on a Musharaka Premise

The client requests the bank for the letter of credit. The bank, in the wake of analyzing the proposal asks the client to deposit his agreement of Musharaka. A letter of credit is then issued by the bank for the import of products.

Application of Musharaka in Farming

This is being constantly tested in Sudan. Farmers are provided tractors, water pumps, sprayers and so on and some working capital for purchase of seeds and pesticides etc. The farmer uses his land, hard work and capital for Musharaka. In return, when the yield is harvested, the farmer gets 30% for his efforts and hard work. The rest of 70% is appropriated between the two parties as indicated by a pre-agreed ratio.

CHAPTER – 33

DIMINISHING MUSHARAKA (HOUSE FINANCING)

It is basically an agreement between two parties to mutually buy an asset. It can be described, from banking point of view, as a situation when a financial institution enters into agreement with a client to acquire an asset. Its actual purpose is not to equally possess the asset for long but the purchaser is anticipated to procure the whole after a certain time period. The importance of Diminishing Musharaka has risen in recent times and it is increasingly being used in housing finance. This form of financing is mostly desired when one party wishes to own some kind of asset or set up a business but does not have adequate amount of funds. It thus takes the help of another party, the financier or bank.

Application of Diminishing Musharaka

According to this concept, an investor and his customer contribute for combined possession of an asset. The share of the investor is more and divided into a number of units. It is mutually decided that the consumer will acquire units of the share of investor one by one with passage of time. Thus, increasing his own share till all units of investor are acquired by him making him sole proprietor of the asset. The contract specifies that borrower will gradually, at specified intervals of time, buy these units until a time comes when he has bought all units originally belonging to the financier. The borrower thus will become the sole owner of asset or business. Until this time comes, both parties, the borrower and the financier, are deemed as joint owners of the asset or the business on a pro rata basis.

Steps in Diminishing Musharaka

The steps involved in a Diminishing Musharaka are outlined below:-

Step 1: The owner of property sells property directly to financier, in whom the legal title to property is vested. The financer pays full price of property to the owner.

Step 2: The financier and customer enter into a partnership to co-own the property (constituted by a Diminishing Musharaka Agreement). The financier and customer agree at the start that their respective shares in property shall be pro-rata, concerning their contributions towards the purchase price paid to owner.

Step 3: The parties also agree that during course of their partnership, which has an agreed date of termination, customer will purchase the financier's share in property in installments and for the price that financier had paid for his share on initial date of acquisition. As the customer increases his share in the property, the financier's share correspondingly decreases by the same amount.

Step 4: In parallel to Diminishing Musharaka Agreement, financier grants to the customer a lease in respect of his share in property. The lease is effective for as long as the financier has a share in the property. The prevailing view of Shariah scholars is that it is acceptable for the rent (payable by the customer) to be a percentage amount of the financier's capital in the partnership benchmarked against LIBOR. The indexation against LIBOR allows the financier to charge a floating rate of rent.

CHAPTER – 34

MODARABA

Introduction of Modaraba

Modaraba is a joint venture where one party (the Rab ul-Mal) gives the resources and other party (the Mudarib) shares its skills and expertise in a business and then profits are shared by both parties at the end. Whatever revenues are earned, are shared among the two parties on a pre-decided basis, although any losses are borne by the resource provider only, such type of contract must indicate how possible income is to be distributed.

The way of Distribution of Profit in "Modaraba"

In Modaraba agreement, a defined proportion of profit is distributed among the participants, equally or in different proportions, mutually decided by parties. The proportion of profit can vary from situation to situation. For example, if the business is done in hometown, 25% of profit is given to the manager but if the business is done in another town 45% of profit may be given to manager.

The Termination of Modaraba Agreement

It is terminated at the expiry of specified period or when either of the two parties informs other party about termination of contract by serving a notice. At the time of termination, all liabilities are paid off and receivables are collected. For determining the value of Modaraba, all assets are liquidated. First of all investor receives back the amount that he/ she had invested. The remaining amount is distributed as profit according to the agreed ratio.

The Application of the Modaraba Models for Financing

Modaraba agreement can be made among the account holders as fund contributors and the Islamic bank as a Mudarib. It may also be made by the Islamic bank as a fund contributor, from its own behalf or on behalf of the account holders etc. As it is a trust-based agreement, the Mudarib is not legally responsible for losses but in case of violation of the obligations of trust or undesirable behavior, funds can be withdrawn from the mudarib as long as they are not completely used. The agreement should stipulate whether the Modaraba is unlimited or limited. Ratio for distribution of earnings/ profits among the parties should also be made part of the agreement. The given ratio can be changed at future dates with the consent of parties.

Difference between "Modaraba" and "Musharaka"

- Investment is a sole responsibility of "Rabb-ul-Mal" in Modaraba but in Musharaka investment comes from all the partners.
- In Modaraba, the Rabb-ul-Mal has no right to participate in the management which is carried out by the Mudarib only but in Musharaka, all the partners can participate in the management of the business and can work for it.
- In Modaraba the loss, if any, is suffered by the Rabb-ul-Mal only because the Mudarib does not invest his own capital. His loss is restricted to the fact that his labor has gone in vain and his work has not brought

any fruit to him. However, this principle is subject to a condition that the "Mudarib" has worked with a due diligence which is normally required for the business. If he has worked with negligence or has been dishonest, he shall be liable for recovery of the loss caused by his negligence or misconduct. While in Musharaka all the partners share the loss to the extent of the ratio of their investment.

- In Modraba, the liability of Rabb-ul-Mal is limited to his investment unless he has permitted the Mudarib to incur debts on his behalf but the liability of the partners in Musharaka is normally unlimited. Therefore, if the liabilities of the business exceed its assets and the business goes into liquidation, all the exceeding liabilities shall be borne pro rata by all the partners. However, if all the partners have agreed that no partner shall incur any debt during the course of business, then the exceeding liabilities shall be borne by that partner alone who has incurred a debt on the business in violation of the aforesaid condition.

- In Modraba all goods purchased by the Mudarib are solely owned by the Rabb-ul-Mal, and the Mudarib can earn his share in the profit only in case he sells the goods profitably. Therefore, he is not entitled to claim his share in the assets themselves, even if their value has increased. But in Musharaka, as soon as the partners mix up their capital in a joint pool, all assets of Musharaka become jointly owned by all of them according to the proportion of their respective investment. Therefore, each one of them can benefit from the appreciation in the value of the assets, even if profit has not accrued through sales.

(Sheikh Muhammad Taqi Usmani)

Uses of Musharaka/ Modaraba

These modes can be used in the following areas (or can replace them according to Shariah rules).

Asset Financing

- Short/medium/long - term financing
- Project financing
- Small and medium enterprises setting up financing
- Large enterprise financing
- Import financing
- Import bills drawn under import letters of credit
- Inland bills drawn under inland letters of credit
- Bridge financing
- LC without margin (for Modaraba)
- LC with margin (for Musharaka)
- Export financing (Pre-shipment financing)
- Working capital financing
- Running accounts financing/ short term advances

Liability Financing

- For current/ saving/ mahana-amdani/ investment accounts (deposit giving Profit based on Musharkah/ Modaraba - with predetermined ratio)
- Inter- Bank lending/borrowing
- Term Finance Certificates and Certificate of Investment
- T-Bill and Federal Investment Bonds/Debenture
- Securitization for large projects (based on Musharkah)

- Certificate of Investment based on Murabaha (Eg: Al Meezan Riba Free)

- Islamic Musharaka bonds (based on projects requiring large amounts - profit based on the return from the project)

Types of Modaraba

There are 2 types of Modaraba namely:

1. **Al Modaraba Al Muqayyadah (restricted Modaraba).** Rabb-ul-Maal may specify a particular business or a particular place for the mudarib, in which case he shall invest the money in that particular business or place. This is called Al Modaraba Al Muqayyadah.

2. **Al Modaraba Al Mutlaqah (unrestricted Modaraba).** However if Rabb-ul-maal gives full freedom to Mudarib to undertake whatever business he deems fit, this is called Al Modaraba Al Mutlaqah. However, Mudarib cannot, without the consent of Rab-ul-Maal, lend money to anyone.

CHAPTER – 35

BAI MUAJJAL (CREDIT SALE)

There is a great difference between Islamic finance and modern finance. In Islamic financial practices, Riba is avoided in compliance with Shariah. The main consideration of Islamic finance is to ensure the benefit of everyone from the transactions and nobody is able to earn unreasonable profits by exploiting others. According to Islamic finance, buyers and sellers, borrowers and lenders, all are to benefit from each transaction. It is quite beneficial for all to have a thorough understanding of Islamic finance and know how these terms can come into play in a typical transaction/ business. One of the subjects of Islamic finance is Bai Muajjal, which is a type of credit sale. It is a specific type of financing technique that has been adopted by Islamic banks.

Introduction of Bai-Muajjal

Bai-Muajjal is a term which has been taken from the Arabic words "Bai'un and Ajalun". The word Bai'un represents buy and sell and the word Ajalun denotes a set time or a set period. "Bai-Muajjal " signifies the sale in which the payment of an entity is made at a future set time. In short, it is basically a credit sale. It can also be defined as an agreement made between a customer and a vendor in which the vendor sells definite goods allowable in the

Islamic Shariah and the law of the land to the consumer at a decided price to be paid at a future time in total or by predetermined installments. The vendor may sell the products as per order and requirement of the customer using this technique. Therefore, it is generally a sale of products on credit by which possession of the products is shifted by the seller/ financial institution to the customer, however, the payment of price by the customer is deferred to a future date.

Characteristics

- It is allowed for the customer to place an order to a seller/ financial institution for buying a product, giving its requirements/ specifications through Bai-Muajjal.
- It is tolerable to get cash/ collateral security to pledge the execution or to cover the damages.
- It is also tolerable to document the liability. The product may be acquired earlier or at the time of signing the contract.
- Stock and availability of products are essential condition for signing this contract. Consequently, the seller/ dealer/ bank may buy product as per requirement of the customer.
- Subsequent to the purchase of product, seller/ dealer/ bank must accept damages of product.
- The seller/ dealer/ bank must send the particular product to the buyer on a specific time and at specific location as per agreement.
- The seller/ dealer/ bank may trade the merchandise at a higher price than the acquisition price to earn revenue/ profit.
- The price once set cannot be altered.

CHAPTER – 36

MUSAWAMA

Introduction of Musawama

Musawama basically explains a deal in which the seller is not forced to reveal the price/ cost paid to generate or acquire the good or service. This is different from Murabaha, where a purchaser knowns the price of the product being purchased by him/ her. Musawama is a universal/ standard type of sale in which cost of the product to be traded is bargained among the seller and the consumer without any reference to the cost paid or price incurred by the previous owner.

Application of Musawama

Musawama is utilized when it is difficult to decide about the price of a particular good or service, or when the good consists of a collection of items. In order to obey Shari'ah, there are various constraints to a Musawama, including:-

- The original asset has to be in existence and in vendors' control at the time of transaction.
- The asset must be of value and usable.
- The deal must happen immediately, future transaction dates are invalid.

Some differences with Murabaha

It is different from Murabaha in respect of pricing procedure. Not like Murabaha, seller in Musawama is not forced to disclose cost of the product which he incurred while acquiring the product/ asset. Both parties would bargain on the cost/ price. All other circumstances pertinent to Murabaha are applicable for Musawama as well.

CHAPTER – 37

HIBA

Introduction of Hiba

The word Hiba represents the donation of an item from which the donor may obtain an advantage. It should be instant and absolute. It is an "unconditional shifting of ownership, made straight away, without any exchange or deliberation, by an individual to another and acknowledged by or on behalf of the receiver". Hiba is basically the financial reward. When funds are used to make profits for the financial institution, the financial institution may propose the client Hiba as a form of appreciations. Hiba is not in any form a type of interest. Hiba is also a monetary gift. A gift is a generic term that includes all transfers of property without consideration. The gift has a much wider scope than Hiba, but the gift is considered to be equivalents to Hiba.

Application of Hiba

No recipient of Hiba can be forced to offer anything in exchange for the gifts. It is universal that the donor and beneficiary concur that few of things will be done for reward, and such rewards terminate under a different condition, known as Hiba-bil-Iwaz or rewards for return. When a bank uses another person's money to generate income for the bank, the bank may offer to his customer

"Hiba" as a form of appreciation. But the literary meaning of word Hiba is the donation of a thing from which the donor may derive a benefit. Hiba is totally based on the bank's discretion, and it is 100% different from interest.

An essential element of Hiba is the declaration, "I have given". According to Islamic Law of gift, it is a part of the law of contract. There must be an offer (Zab), an acceptance (Qabul) and transfer (Qabza) whether moveable or immoveable property made voluntary and without consideration, by one person called the donor, to other called donee and accepted by or on behalf of the donor, must be done during the lifetime of the donor and while he is still capable of giving. If the donee dies before acceptance, the gift is void.

Conditions of the Donor

- The donor must be able to understand the nature of the act and not be subjected to any external influence.
- Must be the owner of property to be gifted.
- Declaration of the donor must be a clear and unambiguous intention of the donor to make a gift.
- The donor must be free of any fraudulent or coercive intention.
- He must have ownership of the property to be transferred by way of gift.
- A gift by a married woman is valid and is subjected to same legal rules and consequences.
- A person, in insolvent circumstances, is also valid provided that it is bona fide and not merely intended to defraud the creditors.

Conditions of the Donee

- Acceptance may be made expressly or implied by conduct.
- An absolute gift to an unborn child is invalid, but if the child is born within six months of the date of gift, it will be valid on the presumption that the child actually existed in the womb of the mother.
- A Muslim may also make a lawful gift to a non-Muslim.
- The Donee must be in existence at the time of giving the gift.
- In the case of a minor, the possession must be given to the legal guardian otherwise the gift is void.
- A gift is a void if the Donee has not given his acceptance.
- The real test of the delivery of possession is to see who (the donor or the donee) reaps the benefits of the property. If the donor is reaping the benefit then the delivery is not done and the gift is invalid.

According to the section 122 of transfer of property Act, 1882: "A gift is a transfer of certain moveable or immoveable property made voluntarily and without consideration by one person called the donor to another called the Donee, and accepted by or on behalf of the Donee".

Parties to a Valid Gift

Donor (Wahib)

- Male or female
- Married or unmarried

- Major (who have attained majority under Majority Act 1875 i.e 18 years or 21 years of age if he/she is under guardian appointed by court)
- Owner of property

Donee (Mohub Lahu)

- Muslim or non-Muslim
- Married or unmarried
- Male or female
- Minor or major
- Disgraceful or well-balanced
- Existence of a beneficiary

Subject Matter (Mouhab)

- Transferable or immovable
- Physical and intangible
- It must be a continuation at the time when the reward is prepared

Essentials of a Valid Gift

- Two parties i.e contributor and beneficiary
- Ability of parties to perform all acts required by law
- Official procedure for creating a reward must be completed

How to formulate legal reward

- The announcement by the contributor of his purpose to make reward.
- Taking (expressed or implied) of the reward by the beneficiary or his representative.
- The assertion must be pursued by the release of ownership.

CHAPTER – 38

WAKALAH (POWER OF ATTORNEY)

Introduction of Wakalah

The Arabic meaning of the Wakalah is an agency. It is an Arabic term that denotes "agency contract", it means to safeguard on behalf of some other person. Lawfully, it means an agreement where an individual designates some other person to perform a certain distinct authorized act on his behalf. It is an agreement of parties which indicates performance of any task or giving any service on other's behalf. A mediator is a person who creates contractual and viable associations among a principal and any third party. An action executed by a mediator in favor of the principal will be considered as action by the principal. Agency is required by the law when a mediator has to execute definite assignments which the principal is unable to execute himself. The requirement for agency occurs where an individual has no aptitude or knowledge to execute a definite action. The key characteristics of an agency agreement are service, depiction and the power to perform for the principal.

Application of Wakalah

The contract of Wakalah is about the provision of services. These services include; sale and purchase, letting and hiring, borrowing and lending, guarantee, pledge, gifts, bailment, taking and making payment and admission and acknowledgment of rights. Banks usually charge cost for the agency services submitted by them in favor of their customers. This type of agreement could be Precise or Common.

The Concept of Wakalah used in Different Meanings

Islamic banks use the concept of Wakalah in various Islamic products such as Musharaka, Modaraba, Murabaha, Salam, Istisna'a and Ijarah. It is also used in payment and collection of trade bills and fund management. A fixed fee is charged by the bank from the agent on behalf of services provided by the bank.

Conditions of Al-Wakalah

- The agent must be someone that is capable of performing the responsibility and fulfill the minimum requirement (being sane, adult and capable of making intelligent decisions).
- The subject matter or business dealings must be clearly specified in the contract by the authorizer.
- It is a legal to entrust certain business dealing with an agent even if the authorizer is capable of performing the same deal himself.
- The authorizer has the freedom to terminate the contract or the service of the agent and the agent could also withdraw from the contract. Except if the responsibility of the agent towards the other party is still pending or his obligation towards the other party has yet to be fulfilled.
- The Wakalah contract ends with the accomplishment of the entrusted tasks or mission.
- It is Permissible to charge some fee or commission on the tasks and works involved in the Wakalah contract.

- It is not permissible to conduct Wakalah for physical devotions (Ibadah) since the objective behind these devotions is to test and act as trial to the believers with the exception of certain prayers such as the Pilgrimage (Hajj), slaughtering animals for sacrifice (Qurbani), distribution of Zakat and Fasting of Kaffarah (on behalf of the dead) as stated in the previous hadiths that support the legality of Wakalah.
- The entrusted agent will not be held responsible for any damage negligence or ignorance on the part of the agent.
- The agent is not permitted to act beyond what he was entrusted for by the authorized in first place except if it is an unlimited agency (Wakalah Mutlaqah).

Usually, agency agreement is not allowable in actions banned in the Shariah or acts of treachery such as pilfering and confiscation of belongings or performing business not based on the Shariah. The agent ought to perform in conformity with the instructions of the principal and take due care. If he is employed to sell supplies in favor of the principal, he cannot acquire these merchandises as a consumer. Likewise, if the principal limits the agent to definite boundaries, the agent is constrained to observe them.

Wakala

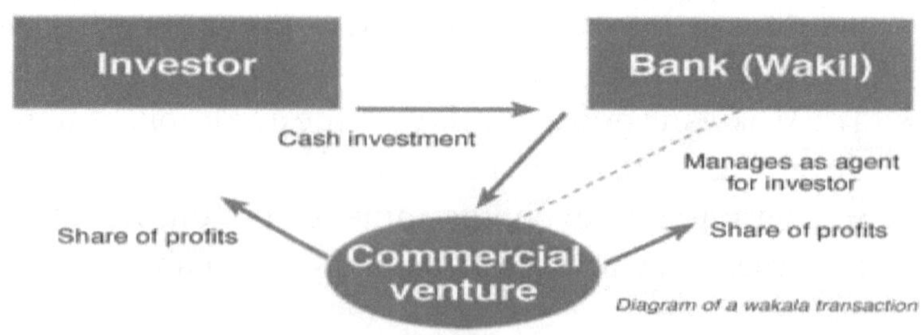

In addition, an agent is not permitted to employ one more agents except he himself is not competent to do it.

According to Hadith:

> Reported by Abu Hurairah (ﷺ) to the effect that: The Prophet (ﷺ) had sent Omar (ﷺ) to be his agent in zakat Collection (representative in zakat collection).

In the case of the sales in Wakalah, the principal assigns an agent to run an assured asset for him. He has the power to negotiate price, implementing the right of choice of terminating a sale on account of faulty merchandises or examination and recurring supplies in addition to similar privileges and liabilities connected with sale deals.

Types of Wakalah

There are two main types:

Wakalah Mutlaqah

It is an unlimited agency or unrestricted Wakalah that is not restricted to any conditions except for those that are permitted in Islam. Also, there is no time limit in this contract. It is not allowable by shariah "fiduciary contract" to mingle Wakalah and personal guarantee (Kafalah) in the same contract at the same time. So according to the shariah, an agent cannot act at the same time as a guarantor because with a nature of fiduciary contracts, such a dual role conflict each other.

Wakalah Muqayyadah

It is a limited agency or restricted Wakalah that is restricted or confined to certain conditions that are allowed by Islam. These contracts are bounded by specific circumstances or time limit. Finally, Wakalah is a not a conclusive agreement; both of parties (principal and agent) may exit at any time by mutual consent. Both parties can also go for one-sided termination or relaxing the compulsion. If the agent terminates an agreement that breaks the terms and conditions of the agency, the agreement is not mandatory on the principal and its soundness depends on his consent.

CHAPTER – 39

WADIAH (SAFEKEEPING)

Introduction of Wadiah

Al-Wadiah is an agreement made by the proprietor (investor) of the assets (the capital) and the guardian (financial institution) for custody. Wadiah is for the protection of deposits/ saving. Such type of contracts do not permit any surplus in addition to the principal amount. The owner of the asset is called Mudi' (Saver), the person delegated with custody is called Wadi' or Mustawda' (guardian) and the asset is Wadiah. Matter of custody is deliberately not mentioned in the Holy Quran while instructions are clearly give in The Holy Qur'an for keeping the trust of others:-

> "Those who are faithfully true to their trusts (Amanah) and to their covenants" (23:8)

Moreover, the Prophet (ﷺ) is reported to have said:-

> "Return the trust to those who entrusted you and do not betray those who betrayed you" (Abu Dawood & Tirmidhi)

Application of Wadiah

In a Wadiah contract, for the safety of our cash and other assets, we deposit money in bank and bank gives a guarantee that it refunds the whole amount or any part of the outstanding amount when the depositor demands it. In such type of agreement, bank acts as a trustee for the deposits.

Types of Wadiah

- Wadiah yad al-Amanah   (Wadiah based on Custodianship)
- Wadiah yad al-Dhamanah (Wadiah with Guarantee)

Wadiah Yad Al-Amana

"Amana" means custodianship, in which the responsibility of guardian is to maintain the deposit/ assets and taking care of the property. Amanah agreement does not create any liability on the custodian in the case of normal loss and damages except in the case of negligence of custodian (fault-based).

Wadiah Yad Al-Dhamanah

It is a combination of two contracts which are safe-keeping (Wadiah) and the guarantee (Damman) contract. The concept of Wadiah is converted into guaranteed safe custody when Damanah contract is attached to a Wadiah contract. The deposited items can be used for trading and other purposes by custodian irrespective of the consent of the depositor as he is guaranteeing the return of the deposit and is liable for any damage or loss. The saver grants the financial institution their consent to make use of the money for rationale use allowed by Shariah. The financial institution in return, assures the custody of the deposit, therefore, making an agreement of Wadiah yad al-Dhamanah. Any income which is derived from the utilization of asset is a right of the custodian. So custodian owns the profit, he may dispose it as he wishes and may give as a gift (Hiba) some portion of profit to the saver.

Conditions

Wadiah has three major parts:-

- Sighah
- Contracting Parties
- The deposit

However, Hanafis state only the Sighah is the only part of Wadiah.

Sighah

From the perspective of applicability of wadiah, the mutual consent/ approval is mandatory. Most of the people say that it is not compulsory. Few people say it is mandatory only if the saver cannot find someone to safeguard his assets.

Contracting Parties

Common agreement holder must have lawful power.

The Deposit

Must be precious and must also be actually acquirable.

CHAPTER – 40

TAKAFUL (ISLAMIC INSURANCE)

Introduction of Takaful

The expression Takaful originated from the word Kafala which is a verb in Arabic and indicates assurance; to assist; to pay attention to one's requirements. It is a classification of Islamic indemnity founded on the code of Ta'awun (joint support) and Tabarru (charitable contribution). In Islam, "Takaful" is basically the concept of insurance which is based on the model of mutual sharing of risk. In this contract, all members of the group provide guarantee to each other. It is based on the principle of shared support. It offers joint security of assets and the property. It is Islamic insurance composed of collection of resources based on the inspiration of joint support. The concept of "Takaful" is based on brotherhood among participants and shared responsibility according to Islamic religious law. In it, participants are mutually responsible to financially help one another if any member among them suffers a loss.

According to The Holy Quran:

> "Basis of Cooperation: Help one another in al-Birr and in al-Taqwa (virtue, righteousness and piety), but do not help one another in sin and transgression". (Surah Al-Maidah, Verse 2)

According to Hadith:

> "We should manage our risk because ALLAH (ﷻ) helps those who help themselves".

Takaful based indemnity is in accordance with Shariah, laws of Islam, and clarifies that it is the duty of person to help and guard each other's benefit. It is formulated on the values of communal conscientiousness, brotherhood, unity and shared assistance.

Working of Takaful

Takaful proposes two major advantages:

- Savings - to secure your future and the future of your loved ones.
- Safety - to save for any future circumstances.

It proposes a variety of investment alternatives to manage your risk, with nearly all flexible compensation alternatives.

Types of Takaful

There are two types of it:-

1. General
2. Family

General Takaful

"In General Takaful financial losses are protected which are likely to arise or caused by events that give rise to legal liability and damage to physical property". Protection on anything other than human life is called general Takaful. It could be applied to your home, car or any other valuables, which depend on what type of Takaful certificate you buy.

Example

- Vehicle against accidental damage or theft.
- Protecting property against fire and theft.

General Takaful involves:

- o Property Takaful
- o Marine Takaful
- o Motor Takaful
- o Miscellaneous Takaful

Family Takaful

For long term security of the family takaful is an Islamic way and it is synonymous with insurance policy.

Family Takaful involves:

- o Group life Takaful
- o Whole life Takaful
- o Endowment Takaful
- o Universal Takaful
- o Marriage Takaful
- o Education Takaful

Difference between Conventional Insurance and Islamic Insurance

Conventional insurance does not comply with the rules and requirements of the Shariah because according to Islamic law these three elements are not conforming.

- Al Gharar (means uncertainty).

- Al Maisir (means gambling).

- Al Riba (means interest).

Al Gharar (Uncertainty)

Gharar is prohibited in Islam, which explicitly precludes exchanges that are considered to have intemperate hazards because of instability.

Al Maisir (Gambling)

In Islam, gambling is forbidden (Arabic: Harām)

They ask you about wine and gambling. Say: 'In them both lies grave sin, though some benefit, to mankind. But their sin is graver than their benefit.' (Qur'an, 2:219 _al-Baqara)

Al Riba (Interest)

Riba (interest, usury) is principally a financial issue in perspective of the way that all religions and mythologies have precluded, limited, debilitated, loathed, or forbidden Riba. Each of the three significant (Ilhami) religions i.e., Islam, Christianity, and Judaism have firmly censured and disallowed Riba in its unique renditions. Later, the priests of Jews and Christian Church relinquished the forbiddance of Riba (investment, usury) that headed the humanity into the monetary turmoil of the present period.

Difference between Takaful and Insurance

- Risk sharing Vs. Risk Transfer
- Wakeel Vs. Guarantor
- Ameen Vs. Owner

CHAPTER – 41

SUKUK (ISLAMIC BONDS)

Based on the definition, "Sukuk can be further defined as a commercial paper that provides an investor with ownership in an underlying asset". It is asset-backed trust certificate evidencing ownership of an asset or its profit (earnings or fruits). In Arabic, another name of the financial security is "Sukuk", in simple words we can say that it is like bonds. Sukuk is a type of bond, which is purely based on Shariah laws, and the principal amount of such bonds prohibits Riba. "Islamic bond" is another name of the Sukuk. It is a bond that produces revenues from the sales, proceeds, or rents without taking an interest. Sukuk is the best way of saving while being in the confines of Islamic laws. It promotes the sharing of risk thus increasing funds mobilization and investment, encouraging appreciation leading to the improved benefits for all.

Role of Security Bonds

According to conventional system, a bond is a form of a loan. It is a negotiable instrument (can be traded in the secondary market), a debt security under which issuer of the bond (Borrower) gets loan according to some terms and conditions. He is obliged to pay the interest (the coupon) at fixed intervals (semiannual, annual and sometimes monthly) and repay the principal at the maturity of bond to the holder of the bond (lender). In case of government bonds, money obtained through bonds is used to finance current expenditure of Government while in case of Private Bonds, bonds provide the borrower with external funds to finance long-term investments.

Difference between Bonds and Stocks

The major difference between Bonds and Stocks is that "bondholders" have a creditor status in the company (they are lenders), whereas stockholders have a partner status in the company (they are owners). Another difference between bonds and stocks is that after a specific time period bond is redeemed (an exception is an irredeemable bond) whereas stock may be outstanding indefinitely.

Issuing Process of Bonds

Public authorities, credit institutions, companies and multinational companies issue bonds in the primary market through "underwriter" (underwriter buys the entire issue of bonds from the issuer and re-sell them to investors). Usually "government bonds "are issued in an auction where members of banks and public may bid for bonds. The rate of Return on the bonds is based on the price of the bond which is paid and terms of the bond (coupon) are fixed in advance and price is determined by the market.

Sukuk (Islamic Bonds)

Sukuk is a plural of Sakk, which means "legal documents, deed, and cheque". It is an Arabic name for the financial certificate but it can be considered as an Islamic equivalent of the conventional bonds. The structure of Islamic finance is based on the asset-backed securities which generate a close association among pecuniary and positive cash-flows. Under this structure, it is a certificate of possession. As a replacement of an interest payment, the investors of the Sukuk collect a profit from the revenue produced by the principal assets.

Islamic mode of financing "Sukuk" have become increasingly popular in the last few years, both for raising government and private finance and every registered/ enlisted company can obtain funds through "corporate Sukuk". These have following characteristics:-

- Sukuk is asset-backed trust certificates.
- Sukuk refers to trust certificates of participation securities that grant investors a share of the asset including the cash flow and risks that commensurate from such ownership.
- Sukuk can be used in several ways so that greater financial flexibility and options can be offered to meet the funding requirements.

In recent years, Sukuk market has grown tremendously from less than $8 billion in 2003 and $45 billion in 2010.

Advantages of Sukuk

- It enhances the investor's liquidity.
- These stocks have high liquidity and can be readily changed into money/ cash.
- It reduces the financing cost and the probability of risk as well.
- It provides the opportunity of changing assets into the securities, therefore serving to the growth of the capital market.

Types of Sukuk

- Sukuk-al-Ijarah (particular ownership of an asset, most commonly used type).

- Sukuk-al-Murabaha (particular ownership of debt).
- Sukuk-al-Istisna'a (particular ownership of a project).
- Sukuk-al-Musharaka (particular ownership of a business).
- Sukuk-al-Istithmar (particular ownership of Investment).

One major drawback of Sukuk is the absence of consistency.

Differences between Conventional Bonds and Sukuk

As compared to the conventional system in which bonds are usually connected to the interest. The holders of the bonds are proposed a definite return on their principal amount. This arrangement abolishes the component of risk. The main focus of the Islamic laws is contribution in both the losses and profits, if any. This condition is equally valid in case of saver bonds. In this case, the investor gives possession of his money which is vulnerable to the both profits and losses. In the bond of a conventional system, the holder of the bond simply obtains a return without any risk. This would be the main discrepancy among Islamic and conventional investments.

Conventional bonds represent the issuer's pure debt but Sukuk represents an ownership stake in an underlying asset. A Sukuk investor has a common share in the ownership of assets; this does not represent a debt owed to the issuer of the bond. So, a Sukuk Investor has a common share in the revenues generated by the Sukuk assets.

CHAPTER – 42

QARD HASSANA (GOOD LOAN)

Qard-e-Hassana is a loan which is made as a gesture of goodwill and the borrower in such type of loan is only required to pay back the borrowed money. On the other hand, the defaulter may have to pay additional money to make up the loss due to delay in return of borrowed money. Most of the people believe that this is the true type of Islamic loan which does not entail Riba, but this type of loan is not advantageous to the creditor. Islamic banks consider that such type of loan is a social security to the people. No individual will go for any criminal activity when he/ she knows that he will be helped at the time of need by an interest free loan. It is very beneficial for the poor and deprived people. This type of loan is basically for people who are jobless or have a very low pay job, who cannot support their family properly, who have some physical disability, or the youngsters who have no guardian and for the widows who have no support from the family.

Islam does not allow usury and considers the money as an item for the purpose of buying/ selling and a way of exchange. Consequently, if you desire to lend money to anyone, then you cannot ask for more than that you have lent.

According to the concepts of commerce, it is truthfully a compassionate finance. The component of kindness is included in the loan of this type. It is an advance which is completely at no cost to the borrower. In Islam, revenue-distribution, on which the viable contract is based, is not a component of this loan, it is mainly for helping and cooperating with those segments of the people that cannot manage to pay interest for borrowing money.

The Holy Quran Says:

> Who is he that will lend to ALLAH (ﷻ) a Qard-e-Hassana so that He may multiply it for him many times? And it is ALLAH (ﷻ) that decreases or increases (your provisions), and unto Him, you shall return. [Surah Al-Baqarah 2: 245]
>
> And give ALLAH (ﷻ) Qard-e-Hassana. [Surah Al-Maidah 5: 12]
>
> Who is he that will give ALLAH (ﷻ) Qard-e-Hassana? For ALLAH (ﷻ) will increase it manifold to his credit. [Surah Al-Hadid 57:11]
>
> Those who give ALLAH (ﷻ) Qard-e-Hassana, it will be increased manifold to their credit. [Surah Al-Hadid 57: 18]
>
> If you give ALLAH (ﷻ) Qard-e-Hassana, He will double it to your credit and he will grant you forgiveness. [Surah Al-Tagaban 64:17]
>
> Establish regular prayer and give regular charity and give ALLAH (ﷻ) Qard-e-Hassana ---. [Surah Al-Muzzammil 73: 20]

SECTION - 09

SPECIAL TOPICS IN ISLAMIC FINANCE

Contemporary Islamic laws are usually analyzed in the light of general guidelines provided to them by Islam. Compliance with Shariah entails all actions to be taken in accordance with the principles narrated in Qur'an and Sunnah and interpreted in Fiqah. The prime guideline is restriction on giving and accepting any investment which is linked with interest, called Riba and staying away from any unnecessary risk, speculations and volatility, called Gharar. Shariah law forbids practices like betting and their financing. In Islamic financing, both risk and return are distributed among all partners associated under an agreement. The fundamentals of Islamic banking are to comply with Shariah laws and no contradiction with regulations and religious convictions of Muslims.

Recently, Development of Islamic Fund has been accomplished through setting up of transitional bodies, for example, Islamic Finance Services Board and Accounting and Auditing Organizations that have helped in setting up bookkeeping practices and necessary arrangements to develop the fund and concerned organizations.

Summary of Islamic Laws and Financial Services

Islamic religious laws/ shariah is the premise of Islamic Fund and all Islamic financial services. These laws advocate practicality and fairness for general public by maintaining moral, social and welfare components of human life. The basis of Islamic banking is on the religion of Islam and it incorporates three essential principles, Akhlaq, Aqidah and Shariah. Aqidah is a belief that obliges a follower not to be in doubt, Akhlaq sets out the moral implicit and explicit rules of how they should live while shariah law oversees all facets of a Muslim's life: socially, politically and financially.

Islamic laws organize human activities and practices by motives behind those activities. Each set of actions and practices has to be in line with commandments of ALLAH(ﷻ). The fundamental source of law is the Quran, which gives rules on how Muslims live, behave and worship. Similarly, the Sunnah also controls all activities in Muslim society including the organization and operation of the Islamic finance. Quran has different verses, which forbid Riba and the same appears repeated in Sunnah. Both have guided Muslims in establishing their management of accounting principles and strategies. Other main sources of Islamic law are Ijma and Qiyas. Sunnah is the vocally conveyed record of the teachings, actions and maxims, silent consents (or disapprovals) of the Islamic Prophet Muhammad (ﷺ), in addition to numerous reports about his companions. Ijma means consensus, that is, acceptance of a matter by a specified group of people, Ijmaa is the term used for an opinion or decision of Islam where all the good and respected scholars of Islam are unanimous in their ruling. For example, there is Ijmaa amongst the scholars that there are five obligatory prayers, or that Adhaan must be given before the prayers, or that a funeral prayer must be organized over a deceased believer, or that swine is prohibited in Islam, etc. Qiyas is the process of logical reasoning in which the teachings of the Quran are compared and contrasted with those of the Hadith. Through this process, the ruling of the Sunnah and the Qur'an may be used as a means to solve or provide a response to a new problem that may arise.

An essential concept in the Islamic finance is an agreement/ contract. An agreement/ contract is an undertaking/ assertion between two parties. The agreement/ contract ought to be binding, legitimate, satisfactory and significant. Contracts are grouped into three classes; invalid, legitimate and void. The Islamic business law is connected with the operations of Islamic way of saving money and it also deals with legal repercussions and contract issues. For the agreement/ contract to be binding and transparent, different conditions ought to be met. There has to be a vendor (the offeror) who makes an offer and a purchaser (the offeree) who accepts the offer. An agreement is possible either orally, written, signed or through an agent/ dealer. There has to be an asset based deal, which has to conform to Shariah laws. The asset must exist at the time of making agreement and ought to be deliverable. All parties must know the details/ particulars of the agreement and nothing should be hidden.

Contract of trade is one of the essential requirements that permits risk free trade of merchandise and property from owner to the purchaser at a cost or deal of exchange. The contract of rent permits a third individual to benefit from someone else's property.

Outline of the Islamic Capital Market

Islamic capital market is one of the key players in the development of Islamic financial foundations in the Muslim world. The basic role of this business is to encourage or permit people, government and organizations with surplus capital to provide the same to others in need. It subsequently helps in balancing out and managing the stream of cash and goes about as a parallel business for alternate sorts of capital markets for capital seekers and suppliers. The beginning of the Islamic capital business sector goes back to the 1970s and 1980s when high net-worth individuals and families were investing their oil profits in investment trusts. By 2008, the Islamic capital business flourished as a result of demand from retailers. Institutional investor is one of the noteworthy donors of the capital for this business.

Islamic capital business sector comprises Islamic money markets, which include organizations that work in confines of Shariah. Incomes originated from trading of prohibited products including pork, liquor and gambling are not considered legitimate in the Islamic capital market.

SECTION – 10

DIFFERENCE BETWEEN ISLAMIC BANKING AND CONVENTIONAL BANKING

In Islam, to distinguish an activity/ practice to be prohibited, hostile, reasonable, beneficial or compulsory generally relies upon an evaluation procedure in the light of Quran and Sunnah. There was no Islamic bank throughout the Prophet's (ﷺ) lifetime, so by no means there can be any example of Islamic financial institution. In the absence of any authentic precedence, these institutions sound like a Bid'a (advancement to the teachings of Islam) but Ijma can grant permission for establishment of Islamic banks.

Starting point of Islamic Finance and Banking

The unique characteristic of Islamic banking is its restriction on premium or interest. Business without utilization of interest bearing loans on Modaraba principles, originates even before the advent of Islam. In pre-Islamic times, Arabs of Mecca composed caravans/ trains of goods to take merchandise to Syria and Yemen. The Meccan merchants frequently utilized agents to transport and trade goods to other areas and come back with profit/ loss which was then distributed according to the principles of Modaraba prevailing at that time. Similarly, when a merchant joined with others to trade together, the profits/ losses were distributed, under an alternate rule called Musharaka, suitable for active participants managing the business jointly.

Restriction on Investment

The Islamic restriction on charging interest (Riba) on loans is well known. Riba is considered haram in Islam. However, to successfully operate, a bank needs to charge a few expenses for its administrations from the users/ clients. For banks, a real part of the profit comes from income that is acquired from charging a premium/ interest. The old terms of Musharaka and Modaraba are present in the advanced Islamic financial framework. They both suggest methods for distributing risk and return at an agreed ratio. Modaraba is utilized for a more uninvolved sort of venture or association, where one group supplies capital or products, and it is the other participant who completes the work required to make profit. Musharaka refers to a more dynamic financing by somebody who is an active participant in the business and a supplier of capital too.

A remarkable contrast of the Islamic financial framework over ordinary banks is on the sharing of risk, which is shared equally by both moneylender and borrower. Although Islamic banks have numerous items like those offered by traditional banks, the two substances differ completely. One key distinction is that ordinary banks earn their income by charging premium/ interest and charges for administrations, while Islamic banks earn their income by profit and loss sharing, exchanging, renting, charging fees for administration and services rendered and utilizing other Sharia compliant trades.

The Supervision of a Sharia Board

A shariah board consists of Islamic researchers who are qualified to give assessments on Islamic business contracts and practices. In an Islamic bank, the board is included the management to verify that all operations are in compliance with Shariah principles. You may ask why a bank needs a Shariah board to guarantee its compliance with Shariah principles. The essential difference between ordinary and Islamic banking is interest free transactions, Islamic banks have to fulfill this prerequisite by simply verifying that none of their transactions include charging a premium/ interest.

Islamic fund is focused on four central principles:-

- Forbidding usury
- Avoiding speculation
- Abstaining from gambling
- Contributing morally

Verifying that Islamic banks agree with Shariah is not simple - thus there is a need for the Shariah supervisory board. This board is the spine of an Islamic bank and assumes a basic part of establishment and working of the bank.

Ideas of Cash and the Premise of Transactions

Islamic banks are not the same as conventional banks because Islamic banks do not charge a premium/ interest. However, this difference is only the tip of the iceberg because the differences are multitude and basics of Islamic financing is entirely different from those of ordinary business of banking.

The essential reason for making an Islamic bank is to propagate and implement Islamic principles of financing. Ordinary banks are profit making institutions and are not focused on religious principles.

Islamic banks focus on Islamic business laws (called Fiqh-ul-Muamalat) for their essential transactions, and they likewise abide by the fiscal laws and regulations of the nations in which they work. On the other hands, ordinary banks focus on a nation's monetary laws and regulations, they do not have contact with any religious body. Islamic researchers perceive that money has a value, however with restrictions.

Associations with Clients

When you deposit your paycheck in a reliable bank, your association with that bank is one of loan provider to debt holder; the bank has an obligation to pay back your cash with or without interest as written in your contract with the bank. Thus, the roles reverse when the bank gives you a credit. The relationship between a client and an Islamic bank is totally different; the indebted person and loan provider relationship does exist in Islamic banking. To comprehend the relationship between the client and Islamic bank, you must recognize the purpose of that relationship that is mutual benefit and facilitation.

Speculations in the Bank

Speculations in reliable business banks are focused around ensured principal amount and getting an agreed amount of profit. For instance, say that a client deposits $10,000 in a six-month term deposit. Following six months, the bank has the obligation, which may be seen as liability, to pay back the client the principal amount in addition to the premium rate charged for six months. Regardless of the possibility that the bank lost the cash in a financing, the bank is still obliged to pay back the interest/ premium.

In Islamic banking, managing an account is a distinct venture. In spite of the fact that the client deposits the cash to acquire additional profit for his funds, his investment and returns are not ensured. Assume the Islamic bank loses cash in an unforeseen business failure. In this situation, the bank is not obliged to pay profit to its client. The key distinction is that Islamic Banking is focused on Shariah compliance. Main principles of an Islamic bank are:-

- The non-attendance of interest based (Riba) transactions.
- The avoidance of monetary practices of persecution (Zulm).
- The avoidance of monetary practices of speculation (Gharar).
- The deduction of an Islamic Tax (Zakat).
- The discouragement of products and services which entails unlawful money (Haraam).

Traditional banking is focused on indebted person and loan provider relationship on one hand, and between the borrowers and the bank on the other. Premium is thought to be the cost of credit, reflecting the open door expense of money.

Islamic law considers a credit to be given or taken, complimentary, to meet any requirement. Hence in Islamic Banking, the leaser ought not to exploit the borrower. When cash is loaned out on the condition of premium/ interest, these types of businesses are using unfair means in the name of business. The Islamic principle underlying for such sort of transactions is "arrangement not unreasonably, and ye should not be managed treacherously" [2:279] which clarifies why business saving money in an Islamic framework is not focused on the borrower bank relationship.

The other rule relating to fiscal transactions in Islam is that there ought not to be any return without taking a risk.

This rule is pertinent to both work and capital. Capital has to be connected to work and there is no profit for capital unless it is exposed to business risk.

Therefore, money related transactions in an Islamic framework have been created on the premise of the aforementioned principles. Thus, financial relations in Islam are participatory in nature.

Conventional Finance/Banking	Islamic Finance/Banking
Relations with its customers is that of creditors and account holders.	Relations with its customers is that of participants.
It gives more prominent stress on lay-away value of the customers.	It gives more noteworthy attention to the suitability of the activities.
It can charge extra cash (punishment) in the event of default.	The Islamic banks have no clauses to charge any additional money from the defaulters. A just little measure of remuneration and these returns are given to philanthropy. Refunds are given for right on time settlement at the Bank's attentiveness.
It does not manage Zakat.	In the cutting edge Islamic saving money framework, it has turned into one of the administratively arranged capacities of the Islamic banks to be a Zakat Collection Center

	and they likewise pay out their Zakat.
It goes for amplifying profits without any limitations.	It additionally goes for expanding profit, however, subject to Shariah limitations.
The financial investor is guaranteed of a decided rate of investment.	Interestingly, it advertises risk offering between the supplier of capital (financial specialist) and the client of deposits (business visionary).
The capacities and working modes are focused on secular standards.	The capacities and working modes are focused on the standards of Islamic Shariah.
While dispensing money account, running back or working capital fund, no understanding for the trade of products and administrations is made.	The execution of assertions for the trade of products and administrations is an unquestionable requirement while dispensing subsidizes under Murabaha, Salam and Istisna's contracts.
Premium is charged even in the event that the association endures losses by utilizing banks reserves. Thusly, it is not focused on benefit and misfortune imparting.	Islamic bank works on the premise of profit and loss sharing. In case, the business has endured losses, the bank will impart these losses according to the mode of account utilized (Modaraba, Musharaka).

The rate of the interest charged on the capital is based on the length of time.	The level of profit is based on the profit earned through trading.
Use of money is as a commodity which leads to inflation in the economy.	Use the money in the economic system through trade related activities for the purpose of proper circulation.
Guarantee all deposits.	Guarantee deposits just for deposit accounts.

References

Bahl, R. W., & Linn, J. F. (1992). Urban public finance in developing countries. The World Bank.

*****